AF531430

EMERGING ENTREPRENEURS

Editors

Dr. S. Maria John
Dr. R. Jeyabalan
Dr. S. Krisnamurthy

DISCOVERY PUBLISHING HOUSE
NEW DELHI

First Published–2004

ISBN: 81-7141-874-0

Published by:

DISCOVERY PUBLISHING HOUSE

4831/24, Prahlad Street, Ansari Road, Darya Ganj
New Delhi–110 002 (India)
Phone: 23279245 • Fax: 91-11-23253475
e-mail: dphtemp@indiatimes.com

Printed at:
Arora Offset Press
Laxmi Nagar, Delhi 110 092.

Preface

The Post-graduate Department of Commerce, Cardamom Planters Association College, Bodinayakanur 625 513 (TN) organized a two-day National Level Seminar titled *"Entrepreneurism in Rural Economy"*. In the seminar, many eminent personalities, Professors of various universities and colleges and research scholars have presented their research articles and papers on matters relating with socio-economic factors affecting entrepreneurship, future entrepreneurism, stress to entrepreneurs the role of Information Technology, entrepreneurship management. Role of Technical Consultancy Organization and the Impact of WTO. Sincere and modest efforts had been taken in the present book by the co-editors viz Dr. R. Jeyabalan and Dr. S. Krishnamurthy, Readers in Commerce, Cardamom Planters' Association College Bodinayakanur to select quality oriented research articles and the same are presented under the title *"Emerging Entrepreneurs"*.

The research articles presented in this book provide maximum possible information useful regarding the subject matter taken up for discussion. This book also sets out to provide its readers the global aspects of entrepreneurism. The perspectives of co-operative entrepreneurism also take a vital part.

We are happy to express our sincere thanks to the honourable management of CPA College, Bodi, the contributors, the participants on the seminar and all our colleagues who supported it on brining this task to a great success. Our earnest thanks are also due to Mr. Tilak Wasan the Proprietor, DPH Publishers and Booksellers, New Delhi for the sincere efforts taken in publishing this book.

Dr. S. Maria John
Dr. R. Jeyabalan
Dr. S. Krisnamurthy

Contents

List of Contributors

Dr. D. Aravazhi Irissappane, Faculty in Commerce, Post-graduate Department of Commerce, Govt. K.M. Centre for Post-graduate Studies, Pondicherry University, Pondicherry-605 008.

M. Balasubramanian, HOD/Commerce, A.K. College of Arts and Science, Krishankoil.

A. Usha Devi, Nadar Saraswathi College of Arts & Science, Theni. II. M. Com.

Mr. T. Palaneeswari, M. Com., M. Phil., Lecturer in Commerce (S.G), S.F.R. College for Women, Sivakasi.

M. Ganesan, C.M.S. College of Science and Commerce, Coimbatore-6.

Kibet Leleito Erick, Erode College of Pharmacy, Erode-638 112.

Haji Dr. M. Sheik Mohamed, M. Com., M. Phil., Ph. D. FICWA, PGDCA, FMSPI, PGDFM, Reader and Head, Department of Commerce, Jamal Mohamed College, Bharathidasan University, Tiruchirappalli-620 020. Tamilnadu.

D. Sugumar, M. Com., Full-Time M. Phil. Scholar, Jamal Mohamed College, Tiruchirappalli-620 020.

R. Pandi, M. Com, M. Phil., Lecturer (S.S.), Government Arts College, Paramakudi, Tamil Nadu.

Dr. N. Namasivayam, Prof. & Head, Department of Commerce, DDE, Madurai Kamaraj University, Madurai 625 021.

Dr. S. Vijayakumar, Lecturer, Department of Commerce, M.K.U. College, Madurai 625 021.

A. Oliver Bright, M. Com., MBA., Co-ordinator, Department of Commerce, St. Thomas College of Arts & Science, New Colony, Koyambedu, Chennai-600 107.

Prof. A. Viswanathan, Professor & Head, Department of Commerce, Kanchi Mamunivar Centre for Post-graduate Studies (Government of Pondicherry) Pondicherry-605 008.

J. Madhi Vani, M. Com I, Nadar Saraswathi, Arts and Science College.

Dr. V. Selvaraj, Reader in Commerce, Nehru Memorial College, Puthanampatti-621 007. Trichy, Tamil Nadu.

Dr. P.M. Meera Mohiadeen, Lecturer (SG) in Commerce, P.G. and Research Department of Commerce, Jamal Mohamed College, Trichy-620 020.

S. Sivakumar, S.G Lecturer & Head, Department of Computer Science, C.P.A. College, Bodinayakanur-625531.

Mrs. A. Mary Grace, SGL in History, J.A College for Women, (Mother Tresa University), Periyakulam-625 601.

Dr. S. Maria John, Reader and Research Advisor, Department of Commerce, C.P.A. College, Bodinayakanur-625 513.

B. Sella Raja, M. Com., M. phil., Lecturer in Commerce, C.P.A. College, Bodinayakanur-625 513.

Dr. E. Mubarak Ali, Dr. A.M. Mohamed Sindhasha, Prof. A.R. Mohamed Ismail, M. Abdul Hakkeem, Jamal Mohamed College, Trichiappalli-20.

Dr. S. Maria John, M.Com., Ph.D., Reader in Commerce, C.P.A. College, Pankajam Nagar, Bodinayakanur-625 513. Theni District.

Dr. K. Andivelu, M.Com., Ph.D., Reader in Commerce, C.P.A. College, Pankajam Nagar, Bodinayakanur-625 513. Theni District.

S. Jegadeesan, II M.Com. CPA College. Bodi Tamil Nadu.

Mrs. Chitra Jeya Murugan, Department of Commerce, Nadar Saraswathi College, Theni-625 531.

Dr. R. Srinivasan, Lecturer, Post graduate Department of Corporate Secretaryship, Bharathidasan Government College for Women, Muthialpet, Pondicherry-605003.

G. Vijay Jesuraj, Research Scholar, Department of Commerce, St. Joseph's College, Trichy.

1

Information Technology and Entrepreneurship Management

Dr. D. Aravazhi Irissappane

Introduction

If we go through the business history of India, we will come across the names of persons who have emerged as successful entrepreneurs i.e., Tata, Birla, Modi, Dalmia, Lijjatt, Kirloskar. These well known names of successful entrepreneurs in the country, who have started their business enterprises in small way have made good fortunes. Success of an enterprise to a great extent, is attributed to the skills of an entrepreneur. What makes the entrepreneurs successful? Do they have anything common in their personal characteristics? Joseph A. Schumpeter, for the first time in 1934, assigned a crucial role of "Innovation" to the entrepreneur in his "Theory of Economic Development". Richard Cantillon, considered entrepreneur as a "risk bearer". Jean Baptiste says entrepreneur could succeed only by acquiring the organizing skill. Of late, a new breed of entrepreneurs is coming to the fore in large industrial organisations. They are called intrapreneurs. They emerge from within the coffins of an existing enterprise. The concept of intrapreneurship has become very popular in developed countries like the USA.

In a conference held in the USA on entrepreneurship, the term entrepreneurship is defined as an attempt to create value through recognition of business opportunity, in the management of risk-taking appropriate to the opportunity.

Entrepreneurship is regarded as closely associated with economic history of India. Information Technology can be traced way back to even as early as Rigveda. India which itself is an under-developed country aims at decentralized industrial structure to mitigate the regional imbalances in levels of economic development, small scale rural entrepreneurship in such industrial structure and plays a crucial role to achieve balanced regional development. I strongly feel that the basic aim of this conference is to analyse the important role that the entrepreneurship plays in the economic development of a rural economy.

Entrepreneurship and Information Technology

The 90s has seen the Information Technology spreading very rapidly and fast among various sections of population across the world. The internet technology in the later part of the 90s has also changed the way people communicate with each other. The coming years would see increasing technology development and focus on what is being called the "ICE Age" (Information Communication Entertainment). When the Information Technology revolution started, the focus was on the segment of people who required in their day-to-day work—Accountants, Designers Industrialists. Developing countries adopted this technology in their own place, as and when the need dictated it. The internet age changed it all to include every one, as connectivity is no longer a luxury (till a few years back, telephone possession was considered just that in India). This has provided the Information Technology industry the opportunity to start a lot of discussions to bridge the digital divide, essentially to expand their markets into those areas/countries, where there was no infiltration of computers during the earlier Information Technology revolution either because there was no need for it or the people there couldn't handle it. This has been duly noticed by the international corporate dependent Community (*UN, WB, etc.*) and promoted with vigour among poor countries.

India is a land of enterprises, where 60% of the population is still self-employed. EDP in India happens in two sectors—organized and unorganized. The organized sector has all the limitations of the red tape and the advantages of resource allocation. The unorganized sector is more dynamic, but has many limiting factors. Here, the individual who has seen the opportunity is the prime mover, but, this industry has played a supportive role of some one who can help the person to go ahead, but, cannot help with the visioning.

There is a definite spread of the Information Technology connectivity in the rural areas, thanks to the enormous funds being made available by the industry at the operation level and the co-operation of the political and the bureaucracy at the policy level. The necessity to make Information Technology sustainable through creation of opportunities has resulted in the creation of Rural Information Technology ventures. The successful businessmen from urban areas have started ventures in rural areas also. The Government is also bending backwards to accommodate the urban businessman in rural ventures. The obvious perks for the business man would include, the "development" value gained through such ventures, the operational cost cutting, the availability of Information Technology, labourers at lesser cost for more hours. This would mean the rural Information technology skilled youth would remain a labourer for the urban businessman. They would be provided jobs in 'Information Technology industry' but would not reap any great benefits. The Government and other institutions have made earnest efforts to create entrepreneurs and wealth centres in the rural areas utilizing the opportunity being presented through the rapid spread of Information Technology with the help of computer institutions. Information Technology would provide them skill-training in launching rural Information Technology enterprises in areas such as management, economic, marketing, etc; hand-hold them through the starting troubles and help them establish and manage a business venture. The entrepreneurs must acquire skills for initiating, managing and sustaining a business. The potential initiator would also be given the market information in the various opportunities such as data processing, accounting software packages etc. The programmes must be designed in such a way that they would also educate the individual entrepreneur to an exercise of visioning and sensitise him/her to the social issues in the area. Every input would be provided to educate the initiator on the fact that of a wealth centre in the rural area for its own developmental work.

The information management has to provide openings to the entrepreneurs in the following:

1. Legal and statutory requirements needed for the starting up of a business venture;
2. Application of Information Technology in the field of Market trends;
3. I.T. business marketing;
4. Business economics and rural economy;
5. Professional approach to project management and stress on process creation and communication;
6. Managing the potential of the people around them, through augmentation of skills and attitudes.

Role of I.T. in Enhancing the Entrepreneurial Skills

Entrepreneur, entrepreneurship and enterprise go hand in hand. In practice, an entrepreneur takes numerous decisions to convert his business idea into a running concern. In setting up a unit, project selection is the first corner stone to be laid down. 'Well begun is half done' A project can be defined as a scientifically evolved work plan devised to achieve a specific objective within a specified period of time. Projects can be classified into Quantifiable and Non-Quantifiable, Sectoral and Techno-economic projects. For the purpose of project identification and selection every entrepreneur should be exposed to the technological innovation in the field of communication and technical support. Project identification is done by generating some project idea. Each of these project ideas are then, evaluated with the help of a tool called 'SWOT' analysis. The Information Technology products will immensely help the entrepreneurs to involve effectively in SWOT analysis.

Normally, small scale enterprise does not include sophisticated techniques which are used for preparing project reports of large scale enterprises. But with the advent of Information Technology these facilities can be practised in the small scale organisations also. A small unit having less capital formation can also involve very much in the process of estimating capital costs, sources of finance, assessment of working capital requirements and other financial aspects such as profitability of the project, projected profit and loss account, Balance sheet, cash flow statement, etc. Further, the Break-Even analysis should also be presented in the project report. With the help of computers the abatement costs, the socio-economic benefit expected to accrue from the project can also be estimated. While framing an implementation scheme one has to involve in Project Evaluation and Review Technique (PERT) and Critical Path Method (CPM) also. The Network analysis, Graphical Evaluation and Review Technique (GERT), Workshop Analysis Scheduling Programme (WAST), Line of Balance (LOB), etc. are possible only with the help of software packages.

Information Technology paves the way for the completion of the appraisal within the shortest possible time. The project appraisal will minimize the risk involved. It is an assessment of a project which includes the following:

Economic Analysis
Financial Analysis
Market Analysis
Technical Feasibility
Managerial Competence

A well equipped entrepreneur can easily select the best one among the alternative projects.

The Management is an art of getting things done through men, machine, materials and money. Next to Men factor, machine plays a crucial role for an effective entrepreneurship management. Almost in all aspects of management Information Technology comes very handy. Let us examine a few cases.

Working Capital Management

Working Capital is that amount of funds which required to carry out the day-to-day operations of an enterprise-whether big or small. The requirement of working capital may vary from enterprise to enterprise depending upon sales, length of operating cycle, nature of business, terms of credit, seasonal variation in the business turnover of inventories, nature of production, contingencies etc. Both excessive and inadequate working capitals are harmful for an enterprise. So working capital needs to be maintained at a proper size. This calls for Information Technology backed working capital management.

Inventory Management

The inventories can be better managed only through mechanized system backed by computer and other equipments. Among the various models, EOQ model, ABC analysis, inventory turnover ratio etc. are considered as very effective from the economy and effectiveness points of view.

Production and Operation Management

In this aspect of management, the most profitable investment opportunity is decided by applying tools like ratios and capital budgeting. Plant location is a strategic one-time decision. While deciding the plant layout, the factors like production technology and product mix, space for maintenance work, scope for future expansion, lighting and ventilation etc. should be considered.

Quality control is also a strategic decision which requires more attention. It is to be designed to take care of the customer complaints. The management must resort to inspection and Statistical Quality Control techniques.

Marketing Management

Technology is a crux of quality and competitiveness. So far the adoption of Information Technology in small industries hampered due to lack of infrastructural facilities on the one hand, and the present investment ceiling of the small scale industry, on the other. But the Government has set up several tool rooms, production-cum-process development centres, regional testing centres and work shops, schemes for regional parks and ISO-9000 etc. The recent communication revolution has offered hi-tech application for market research which is the most cost-effective substitute for exploratory personal visit abroad. As a matter of fact, the conventional method of market explorations through trial and error and private contracts has been replaced by the electronic network exchanging business queries between the trading parties.

Keeping the crucial role of Information Technology in the field of entrepreneurial management a study was undertaken with the following objectives:

Objectives and Methodology

The Present study has made an attempt to ascertain

1. Whether the SSI entrepreneurs feel the stress in management;
2. To find out the extent of practising Information Technology and its impact in management;

3 Whether the influence of technology minimizes the stress factor.

A Case Study with special reference to entrepreneurs of the small scale units situated in the industrial estates in and around Pondicherry was undertaken regarding the Impact of Information Technology on entrepreneurial management. Totally 85 entrepreneurs were contacted for the purpose of this study.

Primary data and secondary data were collected through a questionnaire and from the data available from the Department of Industries, Pondicherry respectively. Convenient sampling was employed while selecting the entrepreneurs.

Table 1.1. Distribution of Respondents Age-wise

Age class interval	*No. of Respondents*	*Percentage*
21-25	4	4.7
26-30	12	14.1
31-35	18	21.2
36-40	21	24.7
41-45	13	15.3
46-50	12	14.1
51-55	2	2.4
56-60	2	2.4
61-65	1	1.1
Total	**85**	**100.00**

It is worth mentioning the among the total respondents 68 respondents are below the age of 45.

Table 1.3 indicates that almost 60% of the sample entrepreneurs have implemented and managed their units with the help of maximum available Information Technology Products.

Table 1.4. Indicates the various kinds of management stress and its impact on the entrepreneurs' performance. The

Table 1.2. Distribution of Respondents Economic and Technical Background-wise

Sl. No.	*Background*	*No. of Respondents*	*Percentage*
1.	Family Business	23	27.1
2.	Technically Qualified	32	37.6
3.	Origin from working class	18	21.2
4.	Origin from White Collar	5	5.9
5.	Others	7	8.2
	Total	**85**	**100.00**

Table 1.3. Information Technology Application

Sl. No.	*Usage of Information Technology*	*No. of Respondents*	*Percentage*
1.	20	23	27.1
2.	40	32	37.6
3.	60	18	21.2
4.	80	5	5.9
5.	100	7	8.2
	Total	**85**	**100.00**

Table 1.4. Management Stress Factors faced by Entrepreneurs

Sl. No.	*Nature of Stress*	*Entrepreneurs Ranking*			*Weighted Score*	*Rating (Present)*	*Ranking*
1.	Project Management of Working Capital Management	30	27	21	165	32.35	I
2.	Inventory Management Production & in Operation Management	27	22	18	143	28.04	II
3.	Marketing Management	10	14	17	75	14.71	IV
4.	Human Resource Management	12	13	16	78	15.29	III
5.	Total Quality Management	6	9	13	49	9.61	V
	Total	**85**	**85**	**85**	**510**	**100.00**	

application of Information Technology in the field of Project and Working Capital Management has reduced the strain and stress on the entrepreneurs.

Table 1.5. Information Technology and Stress

Sl. No.	*Usage of IT Percentage*	*No. of Respondents*	*Stress Weighed Score*	*Arrearage*
1.	20	23	191	27.1
2.	40	32	131	37.6
3.	60	18	122	21.2
4.	80	5	55	5.9
5.	100	7	11	8.2
	Total	**85**	**510**	**100**

Table 1.5 exhibits very clearly that the stress factor has gone down considerably when Information Technology is practised.

Summing up

The study is undertaken with the intention to substantiate the belief that every entrepreneur of a SSI is undergoing tremendous amount of stress in the absence of full automation and application of Information Technology in the various aspects of management. It is assumed that, if the Information Technology products are used in the various spheres of entrepreneurial management the risk element can be kept at its low. Further, the history reveals that SSIs are more prone to sickness compared to large scale industries. Having kept this factor as the prime mover, the study made an attempt to prove that the Information Technology products minimise the stress element which will pave way for the success of the SSIs.

For this purpose, the study considered both primary and secondary data. Out of the 85 respondents only two women entrepreneurs participated in the exercise. The conspicuous absence of women is mainly attributed to the Indian culture which largely restricts the women's entry into entrepreneurship.

Findings

Nearly 24.7% of respondents are between the age group of 36-40. This suggests that the propensity to assume the entrepreneurial skill should be the maximum in the prime working age which tends to decline with the advancement in age. Only 18-8% of the respondents are from business community. The economic and technical schedule indicates that 37.6% of the respondents are technically qualified to assume. The position of an entrepreneur, while scanning through the stress factors, machinery and other related equipments, marketing and competition, financial management are some of the complicated areas where the entrepreneurs faced an uphill task of managing. Further, the outcome of the study very clearly indicates that the entrepreneurs who were well equipped with Information Technology related products have faced all risks and obstacles and have come out successful.

Suggestions

1. At present Government of India in collaboration with the State Governments in conducting special Computer Training Programmes for the educated unemployed rural youth. Such programmes should be conducted with the involvement of Village, Town Panchayat Presidents and the Chairmen of Municipalities to make it more effective and meaningful.

2. We could notice a gradual increase in the use of Information Technology in Government, Public Sector, Private Sector, Universities, Schools and Colleges. With the setting up of the National Association of Software and Services Corporation (NASSCOM), the country can develop human capabilities in the field of Information Technology.

3. As per NASSCOM study the number of Personal Computers in India is likely to go up from 4.3 million

as on 31.3.2000 to 20 million in 2008. The number of internet subscribers is likely to increase from 0.77 million to 35 million. The internet users may go up to 100 million. Due to this prospective leap in the field of Information Technology, the industries must take necessary steps to improve the entrepreneurial skills among the citizens of our country.

4. A common man in this country is largely unaware of the potential and use of Information Technology in his day-to-day life. This acts as a retarding factor to the use of Information Technology tools and services by the human resources in India. A mass campaign should be launched to increase awareness.
5. In the field of training the Information Technology industry has contributed 331 crores i.e. 5.2 percentage in the overall growth of the various components of Information Technology industry. In the year 2001-2002 the percentage has come down to 4.6%-(Source-NASSCOM). This is due to the sluggish Information Technology market throughout the world. The Govt. must frame a unique strategy to develop its human resources in the field of Information Technology. Its concentration on Software, Hardware, Peripherals and Maintenance networking etc. should continue.
6. The Government has to encourage Private Software Technology Parks.
7. Zero percent customs and excise duty on Information Technology software may help everyone to have access to computer.
8. The Government should extend income tax exemption to software and service exports.
9. The Govt. should set up more centres for excellence in e-commerce, e-governance, e-CRM.
10. The cyber laws recently framed should be made more flexible.

11. The Government should earmark 1-3 percent budget for every ministry-department for Information Technology applications.
12. Net working should be created in all Universities and Research institutions.
13. The Government must encourage and invest in developing the computer skills in rural entrepreneurs through their own mother tongue.

References

Desingu, Setty E:, *Developing Entrepreneurship among women, Man and Development,* Vol. 2, No. 3, September 1980.

Hanna N and Dugonjic V:, *A National Strategy of Exploitating Information Technologies"* in UNCTAD, Advanced Technology Assessment System.

Jeemol, Unni and Uma Rani, *"Globalisation, Information Technology Revolution and Service Sector in India,* Journal of Labour Economics, Oct-Dec 2000.

Joshi, Arun:, *Lala Shriram: A study in Entrepreneurship and Industrial Management.*

Khankar, SS:, *Entrepreneurship in Small-Scale Industries,* Himalayan Publishing House, New Delhi, 1990.

Planning Commission, *Mid-term Appraisal of Ninth five year plan* (1997-2002).

Rao, B.S.V., *Entrepreneurship Development among Technical Personnel, A few observations,* SEDME, September, 1983.

World Bank:, *World Development Report 1999-2000, Entering the 21st century-2000.*

2

Factors Influencing Entrepreneurs in Rural India

M. Balasubramanian

According to Noah Webster, entrepreneur is "one who assumes the risk and management of business."

The term entrepreneur meant an individual providing the fourth factor of production namely enterprise.

As the family is the basic unit for social organization, so the enterprise is the basic unit for economic organization—in course of time, enterprise was finally separated from that of supplying resources, but the entrepreneur continued to remain identified with the owner.

The functions are as follows:

(i) Perceiving market opportunities.

(ii) Gaining command over scarce resources

(iii) Purchasing input

(iv) Marketing of the products and responding to competition.

(v) Dealing with the public bureaucracy (concessions, licenses and taxes)

(*vi*) Managing human relations within the firm

(*vii*) Managing customer and supplier relations

(*viii*) Managing finance

(*ix*) Managing production (control by written records, supervision, coordinating input flows with orders, maintenance)

(*x*) Acquiring and over seeing assembly of the factors

(*xi*) Industrial engineering (minimizing inputs with a given production process)

(*xii*) Upgrading process and product quality and

(*xiii*) Introducing new production technique and products

The factors behind entrepreneurs in Rural area are as follows:

1. Entrepreneurial ambitions:

(*a*) To make money

(*b*) To continue family business

(*c*) To secure self employment/independent living

(*d*) To fulfil desire of self/life/parents

(*e*) To gain social prestige

(*f*) Other ambitions—making of a decent living, self-employment of children, desire to be something creative, provide employment to others, circumvent Land Ceiling Act, etc.

2. Compelling reasons:

(*a*) Unemployment

(*b*) Dissatisfaction with the jobs so per held on occupation pursued

(*c*) Make use of idle funds

(*d*) Make use of technical/professional skills

(*e*) Others—maintenance of large families, revival of sick unit started by father, etc.

3. Facilitating factors:

(*a*) Success stories of entrepreneurs

(*b*) Previous association (experience in the same of other line of activity)

(*c*) Previous employment in the same or other line of activity

(*d*) Property inherited/self acquired/wife's

(*e*) Advice or influence (encouragement) of family members/relatives/friends

(*f*) Other-association as apprentices and sleeping partners

AD Mc Crory observed the dreams of the entrepreneurs appeared to be not to "get rich but to get big."

The main qualities may be made on entrepreneur

(*a*) Capacity to assume risk and processing self confidence

(*b*) Technological knowledge, alterness to new opportunities, willingness to accept change and ability to imitate.

(*c*) Ability to marshal resources

(*d*) Ability of organization and administration

Emerging Class an Entrepreneur

A number of talented persons from the corporate world in America are learning their jobs to start their own manufacturing/business units because their management are not receptive to new ideas.

The idea was promising and the opportunities awaiting entrepreneurs inside large corporations could be tremendous provided it could be made unable.

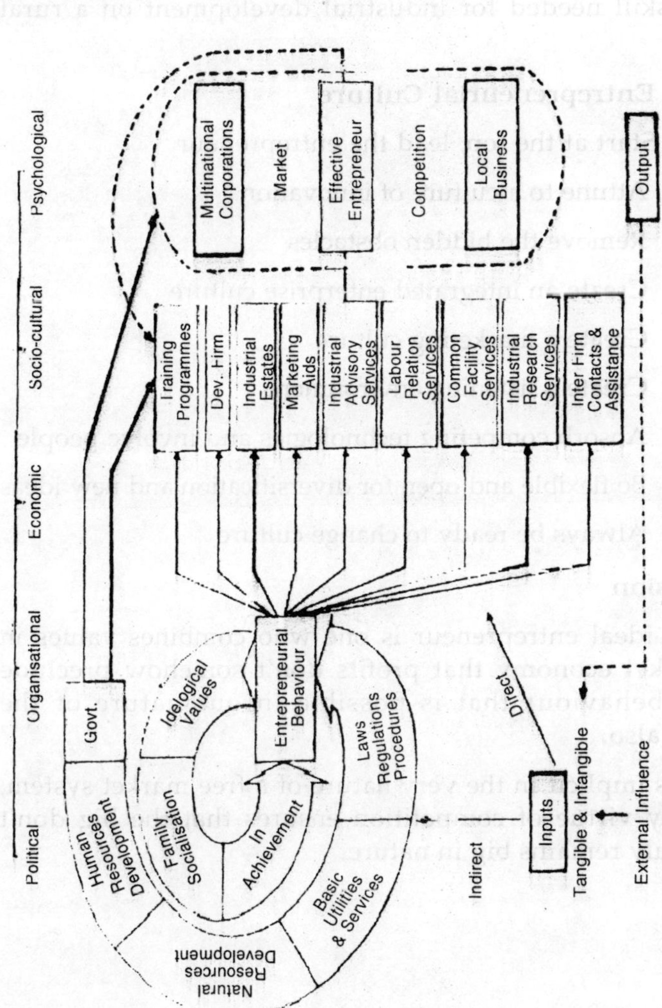

Fig. 2.1. A Model of Factors Influencing the Emergence of Entrepreneurship

Source: Adapted from Abdul Aziz Mahumud "Developing Effective Indigenous Entrepreneurs", Malaysian Management Review, April 1974, Vol. 9, No. 1.

A dynamic organization needs its ideal men, its creative thinkers, its people who can plan and initiate changes—the organizational ability is probably the most critical skill needed for industrial development on a rural area.

Change Entrepreneurial Culture

1. Start at the top, lead the entrepreneur
2. Attune to a culture of innovation
3. Remove the hidden obstacles
4. Create an integrated enterprise culture
5. Create a marketing culture
6. Create a listening environment
7. Absorb competing technologies and involve people
8. Be flexible and open for diversification and new ideas
9. Always be ready to change culture

Conclusion

An ideal entrepreneur is one who combines values in the market economy that profits don't somehow preclude ethical behaviour that is possible in our nature of the product also.

It is implicit in the very nature of a free market system, which by virtue of competition ensures that the big don't necessarily remains big in nature.

3

Emerging Entrepreneurs in Rural India

A. Usha Devi

Introduction

Works becomes a part of one's life. People involve themselves in some work or other. Some people work for others and some are self employed. The people who work for themselves are called entrepreneur. These entrepreneurs are the backbone for the economic development of a country.

Meaning of Entrepreneur

The word entrepreneur is derived from the French verb "Entreprendre", which means "to undertake". The term entrepreneur has been attributed to all small Industrialist. Entrepreneur is thus a person who organizes and manages an activity or organisation, undertaking the risks for fulfilling some of his needs. His job involves the quality of boldness, courage, dynamism and risk-taking in sufficient measure.

Meaning of Rural Area and Rural Entrepreneurship

Village or town with a population of 20,000 and below are known as rural area. Rural entrepreneurship has been advocated to reduce pressure on agriculture curb emigration of rural people, disperse large scale industrialization, reduce investment cost and generate employment in mass scale for skilled and unskilled persons of the community and reduce regional disparity.

Need for Entrepreneurship in Rural India

Over 74% population of India lives in rural areas. A majority of them, nearly 80% are engaged in agriculture. As a result on growth of economy, the share of agricultural employment is expected to comedown to 60% by 2000-2001 whereas the rural work force is growing at 1.8% p.a. Additionally, the strength of rural population are:

- a large and growing reservoir of potential workers.
- Abundant resources of raw-materials (agricultural produce, agro wastes, forest produce, livestock, mined, materials, etc.)
- traditional skills and capacity for initiation of viable small enterprises and
- large and increasing demand for goods and services

The above scenario calls for increased efforts on economic development of rural areas. The individual as an entrepreneur is a critical factor in economic development and an integral part of socio-economic transformation. Therefore the basic concept of entrepreneurship can notes effectiveness urge to take risks in the face of uncertainties and intuitions. However emergence of an entrepreneur in the society depends closely upon the interlinked social, economic, cultural, religious and psychological variables. Realizing that agriculture sector alone cannot reduce rural poverty on a sustained basis, government initiated several programmes to directly provide employment and attack the problem of rural poverty.

Existing Entrepreneurs in Rural India

There are many entrepreneurs already existing in rural India. They are engaged in following types of works.

A. *Pottery Industry*

Village pottery is one of the oldest crafts that man evolved at the dawn of civilization. About 15 lakh potters are engaged in the manufacture of pottery items in the unorganized sector. Their livelihood depends on pottery as their main occupation. The potters employ traditional skills for making a large variety of earthenwares required for domestic use and other purposes in and outside the village.

B. *Weaving*

Before independence rural people were fully engaged in this craft and they were living happily. They were getting cotton from the village itself. At that time the government was also providing them with raw-materials at control rates and the product was taken as soon as it was ready, with adequate price. There was also a demand for this product in rural markets and in the villages. In recent years the picture is altogether different. All these traditional crafts are in the process of steady decadence.

C. *Tailors*

As profit is more in tailoring, some of rural people became tailors. These new entrepreneurs are semi-skilled and 90% of them are Muslims. To some extent there is innovation and risk-taking attitude in this people. There is scope for tailors, since the readymade garments are in demand everywhere to solve immediate needs. So they need modern skills in order to fulfill the wishes of the target.

D. *Blacksmiths*

Almost every village has blacksmiths who are mainly engaged in traditional hereditary occupation. The same artisan often performs the functions—carpentry and Blacksmithy. Even one started cycle-repairing too. They are generally bound by contractual arrangement for which they are paid in kind. Their activities include manufacture, maintenance and repair services. They are required to service ploughs and agricultural implements etc.

E. *Gem Cutting*

Gem cutting which is defined as an art of artificial diamond making is one such industrial activity which can be promoted at the household level. The traditional gem processing used natural stores which were cut and polished but there was no attempt at calibration or following standard sizes. The modern gem processing differs from the traditional gem and jewellery crafts and many of the new entrants have not come from the traditional jewellery-making communities, but have to undergo formal training. Thirupanjeeli village in Lalguidi taluk has been concentrated with more number of gem cutting units in Tiruchirapalli, so this area has been selected were most of them have undergone training at Trichy Gem Park (TGP) in collaboration with District Rural Development Agency (DRDA).

F. *Cottage Industry*

Many of the rural people are engaged in small scale industries such as.

(a) Synthetic beverages, syrups and sharbats

(b) Pickles

(c) Jam, Jellies

(d) Tomato products, ketch up and sauces

(e) Chutneys

(f) Canned and bottled fruit juices and pulps

(g) Frozen fruits and vegetables

Emerging Entrepreneurs in Rural India

Science and technology has played a positive role in contributing to the development of agro based, forest based, fruit based, livestock based and demands based products. The knowledge level of the masses is not up to the mark to know that new techniques for adopting rural oriented industries. On the other hand, entrepreneurship in the form of small business, trade, sales, petty repair, contractual labour has expanded due to industrialization and development in agriculture. New vistas of rural industrialization have thus been opened up. The salient ones are briefly described as under:

1. Food Processing Technologies

Today, India has become the largest producer of milk in the world. It has also emerged as the second largest producer of fruits as well as vegetables with annual production of 43 and 86 million of tones respectively. The country has entered in to an era of surplus in foodgrains with production grossing 204 million tones in 1999-2000. With the array of natural products, cultivated through varied agro-climatic conditions the agro-processing sector has to play a primary role in economic-development. A few important technologies developed for small—cottage sector are:

A. Mini Rice Mill

A mini rice mill has been developed which saves on valuable rice bran that provides 14-18 per cent edible oil. In addition, brokens are reduced to 0.5 percent and milling time reduced by 25 per cent.

B. Mini Wheat Mill

It provides atta, suji, maida and bran simultaneously. So far, suji and maida are manufactured in large mills requiring high capital and sophisticated technology. Due to mini wheat mill, the production cost is reduced.

C. Speciality Crops

There is an ever increasing demand for natural plant material for use in the manufacture of drugs, pharmaceuticals, cosmetics, food flavours, perfumes, soaps, paper pulps, other industrial products and as fuel, timber etc. cultivation and processing of these plants has considerable potential as a small scale Industry. In addition, wastelands can also be brought under cultivation. Depending upon land holding, processing can be taken up on individual or co-operative basis and in the industrial sector. Some of the important plants are listed below:

(a) Medicinal Plants

(i) Discorea Deltoidea and D. Floribunala

Raw materials for diosgenin for further synthesis of steroidal drugs

(ii) Solanum Khasianum

A source of solasodine for production of steroidal drugs.

(b) Essential Oil Bearing Plants

(i) Lemongrass;

Used in flavouring cosmetics, soap, perfumery, synthesis of ciltral needed in the manufacture of Vitamin A and a number of aromatic compounds.

(ii) Java Citronella

A source of perfumery chemicals like citronellal and geranoil, needed in soap, perfumery and flavouring industry.

(c) Other Economic Plans

(i) Jojoba

A desert crop oil valuable as lubricant for high speed machines, hair restorer and in cosmetics.

(ii) Salvadora Persica

Drought resistant plant, seed oil is a good substitute for coconut oil.

3. Leather and Animal Waste Based Technologies

Leather processing is another important area which is largely in the hands of unorganized sector and technology upgradation can make a marked impact on value addition. Some important innovative technologies available in leather processing are:

(i) Wet Blue Chrome Processing

It is a technology that brings in market improvement in the traditional cottage tanning operations. It results in upgraded product quality as well as saves on processing time. The raw hides thus tanned can be further processed into chrome tanned leather.

(ii) Milled Grain Side Leather

It is a buffalo hide based leather used for making travel goods; ladies hand-bags and shoe uppers rural tannery equipment is used.

4. Low Cost Building Materials Components and System

Shelter is one of the basic need of a human being. Construction materials and components have a vast market which has further gone up in recent years with emphasis on shelters for economically weaker sections under various welfare schemes. Rural artisans can play a vital role in taking up activities related to their manufacture, marketing and laying new system. Some of the technology Innovations in the manufacturing area are:

(i) Brick Moulding

A simple hand molding table has been developed that moulds bricks in accurate shape and size. This device can mould 1000-1500 bricks a day improved dimensional accuracy savings in mortar consumption.

(ii) Precast Stone Block

Precast stone block masonry i.e. an economical substitute for random rubble masonry. The blocks of standard size are made for cement concrete mix and stone pieces up to 25cm size.

(iii) Drinking Water

A large number of our villages still do not get adequate supply of potable water. A sizable requirement is met from ground water sources an account of indiscriminate utilization of this important resources both the quality and supply position has been deteriorating. Technologies have been developed for purification quality assessment and storage of water listed below are some of the salient ones.

(iv) Ground Water Exploitation

Wells have been used as sources of water supply. Since time immemorial locating the correct spot for exploration of ground water has remained a tricky business. Today a simple technology is available where ground water exploration is possible with 95 per cent success ratio.

(v) Water Filter Candles

Water filter candles as used to domestic water constrainers including earthen pitcher, can meet the daily requirements of safe drinking water for an average family.

(vi) Environment and Sanitation

The need for low cost sanitation system is well known. Artisans can play a vital role in practicing new techniques in the disposal of waste water through brick insitu system or new soak pit models, sanitation devices as wells manufacture of low cost stone sanitary-ware. A large number of new technology options are available.

(b) Upgradation of Artisanal Skills

(i) Floral Crafts

There is a good demand for floral handicrafts made out of dehydrated flowers and foliage. The arrangement of dehydrated flowers and foliage in sealed transparent glass or plastic jars makes very good decoration pieces with a potential market demand.

(ii) Brass Metal Crafts

The brass metal craft for making pitcher tumbler, images and Dokra novelty items is one of the old industries. The improved process effects substantial reduction in fuel consumption with higher productivity.

5. Technologies for Other Cottage Industries

There are large number of other technologies that are relevant to the small sector. These include: Production of plant leaf based food containers, multi-fuel, energy-efficient, cook stoves, plastic slates, paper slates, dustless chalk, hand made paper, rope etc.

Conclusion

To conclude, in rural India there is a lot of manpower in the articinal skill. These can be improved further due to the development of science and technology. For the sufficient earnings in their day-to-day life, they can become new entrepreneurs getting financial assistance from the government. As India's major portion lives in rural India, the development of these people will ultimately result in the economic development of India.

4

IT Entrepreneurship Management in Digital Era

Mrs. T. Palaneeswari

Introduction

Change is constant and is inevitable. Digitalization has brought in a revolution in the world where everything seems to be e-enabled. Business in the Information Age must compete in a challenging market place—one that is rapidly changing, complex, global, hyper-competitive and customer-focused. The revolution in business caused by the Internet and its related technologies demonstrates that Information Technology (IT) is essential ingredient for the success of today's internet worked business enterprise.

Entrepreneurship

An enterprise comes into existence only because of the efforts put in by a person, who would be prepared to shoulder the responsibility of taking the enterprise with him. Entrepreneurship is meant the function of seeking investment and production opportunity, organizing an enterprise to undertake a new production process, raising capital, hiring labour, arranging the supply of raw materials, finding site, introducing a new technique and commodities, discovering new sources of raw materials and selecting top managers for day-to-day operations of enterprise.

Entrepreneurship Management and IT

Management is a multipurpose organ that manages a business and manages managers and manages worker and work. But the functional areas of management in the business enterprise that are of special interest to the entrepreneurs are as follows:

- Marketing and Sales function
- Accounting and Finance function
- Production and Operation function
- Human Resources Management function

IT—the fusion of computing and communications—is creating far-reaching changes in the way we work, the way we live and even in the way we think. IT is a priceless resource, one of which entrepreneurs must take advantage. Small entrepreneur who own computers with internet technologies consider them a valuable tool as it improves productivity and efficiency. Information Technologies including Internet based information systems are playing a vital and expanding role in entrepreneurship management.

IT Marketing and Sales Function

Customer Service

1. **Customer Profiles.** Service to customers is of prime importance to any business. IT can help create customer databases of both existing and potential customers which can be easily accessed and stored for direct mailing.

2. **Customer Contact and Promotion.** Electronic kiosks, one of the IT tools enables a business enterprise to establish and maintain electronic contact with the potential customers. The electronic contact could be made quite interactive which is possible 24 hours a day on all the 365 days which helps a lot in converting a query into a sale.

3. **Targeted Advertisement on the Web.** Web is an economical advertising medium which is more effective in terms of drawing attention of the potential customers from all over the world.

Telemarketing

IT supports all the telemarketing processes that use telecommunication and information systems to execute a marketing programme for customers who want to shop from their homes.

Distribution Channels Management

1. **Delivering Management.** The most sophisticated tracking systems are used to monitor the delivery times, since only fast and accurate delivery times guarantee high customer satisfaction and repeat business.
2. **Improving Sales at Retail Stores.** Self Check-out technology may be used at the retail store to reduce the number of sales people and to provide more information about the product at the shop to the customers.

Marketing Management

1. **Pricing.** Sales volumes are largely determined by the prices of products or services. Online analytical processing supports pricing decisions.
2. **Salesperson Productivity.** Salesperson productivity can be greatly increased by Sales Force Automation available on the Internet which shortens the sales cycle, increases revenue through targeted marketing and enhances order management.
3. **Sales Analysis and trends.** Identification of fast moving and slow moving items, monitoring trends in product profitability, demand and sales life cycle are very convenient with IT infrastructure.

4. **New Product Development.** Present day IT infrastructure offers information regarding the risk profile, cost structures, revenue estimates etc. of proposed products that enables the marketing manager to make an informed choice regarding the product differentiation and launching of new products in the market.

IT in Accounting and Finance Function

General Ledger Accounting Information

IT infrastructures are quite nature in well-managed enterprises with regard to automation of invoicing, debtors accounting, and other related operations.

Financial Planning and Budgeting

1. **Financial Forecasting.** Use of modern IT infrastructures has made it possible to develop real time flexible budgets and to employ more sophisticated budget analysis models in designing annual budget that allocates the financial resources among all activities that best support achieving the organization's goals.
2. **Cash and Fund Flow Management.** Advanced techniques for modeling of cash management can help in ensuring that there are funds just enough to meet the requirement and also in estimating the demand and availability of funds from various sources.

Financial Controls

1. **Budgetary Control.** The modern sophisticated software enables the finance manager to compare the actual performance with the budgeted ones and to tie expenditures to programme accomplishment.
2. **Auditing.** The major purpose of auditing is to ensure the accuracy of financial reports. More sophisticated

intelligent systems uncover fraud by finding financial transactions that deviate from previous payment profiles.

3. **Financial Analysis.** Spreadsheet programme can be used in financial analysis to analyze the financial health of corporations.

4. **Cost Analysis.** Automatic generation of cost variance reports helps the managers to get more insight into the changing business situations and offers leads for identifying opportunities for reduction of costs and improves profitability.

5. **Profitability Reporting.** IT infrastructure can provide a platform for effective responsibility accounting and reporting of profitability of each of the organizational units separately.

IT Production and Operation Management

Materials Management

Materials management deals with ordering, purchasing, inspection and maintenance of materials which can be supported by IT infrastructure. Purchasing can use EDI to place orders. Scanners and voice technologies can support inspection. Robots can perform distribution and materials handling. Inventory software automatically generates a purchase order when the inventory falls to the reorder point. Quality control software provides information about the quality of the raw materials as well as finished products.

Production Planning/Operations

1. **Materials Requirement Planning (MRP).** In many manufacturing systems the demand for some items can be interdependence. In such a case MRP software facilitates the plan for acquiring all such items. 'Just-in-time'; technique can be used to minimize inventory

levels only under conditions of highly connected procurement environment.

2. **Project Management.** A project is a one time effort composed of many interrelated activities. The management of projects is enhanced by Project Management Techniques such as PERT and CPM which schedule activities in an optimal sequence.

Automatic Design Work and Manufacturing

1. **Computer Aided Design (CAD).** CAD helps in creating, simulating and evaluating models of product designs and manufacturing processes and facilities.

2. **Computer Aided Manufacturing (CAM).** CAM uses computers and robots to fabricate, assemble and package products, to monitor and control the production process.

3. **Computer Integrated Manufacturing (CIM).** CIM is a tool that facilitates simplification of all manufacturing technologies, automation of as many of the manufacturing processes as possible, integration and coordination of all aspects of design, manufacturing and related functions.

IT in Human Resources Management

Recruitment

1. **Man Power Planning.** Recruitment is finding employees, testing them and deciding ones to hire. IT can help an enterprise to keep a track of the right people in and outside the organization.

2. **Recruitment and Selection.** IT helps in the management of resumes received at regular intervals from different sources like employee referrals, consultants etc. and helps in getting the best set of resumes for short-listing candidates for selection.

Human Resources Maintenance and Development

1. **Training and Development.** With the help of Multimedia and simulation techniques, it is now possible for an enterprise to train their employees for different jobs.

2. **Performance Evaluation.** IT has made the performance appraisal more regular, systematic and comprehensive. Wage and Salary review is related to performance evaluation and can be handled by IT applications.

Human Resources Mangement and Planning

1. **Personal Files and Skills Inventory.** All information about a person is contained in a HRM Personal files when the personal files are computerized, it is easy to identify qualified employees for promotion, transfer and special training programmes.

2. **Compensation and Incentive Planning.** IT tools help in analyzing the range and distribution of employee compensation, like wages, salaries, incentive payment, fringe benefits etc.

3. **Personnel Planning.** The human resource development forecasts requirements for people and skills.

4. **Labor-Management Negotiations.** Labour-management negotiations can take several months during which times employees may present management with a large number of demand. Group Decision Support System have helped improve the negotiation climate and reduced the time needed for reaching an agreement.

5. **Government Reporting**. IT enables the managers to keep track of the statistics and produce reports required by a variety of government laws and regulations, regarding employee health, work place hazards, accidents and safety procedures.

IT Tools

IT tools that facilitate the above major functional areas of enterprise management are as follows:

Computer Hardware

Software

- System Software
- Application Software
  - Spreadsheets
  - Graphics
  - Word processing
  - Multimedia
  - Database Management
  - Communications
  - Desktop Publishing
  - Group-ware

Electronic Communication Tools

- Electronic Mail
- Paging
- Voice Mail
- Internet Phone Systems
- Faxing
- Electronic Data Interchange
- Web Publishing

Electronic Conferencing Tools

- Data and Voice Conferencing
- Video Conferencing

- Tele-conferencing
- Discussion Forums
- Usenet Newsgroups
- Chat Systems
- Electronic Meeting Systems

Collaborative Work Management Tools

- Calendaring and Scheduling
- Task and Project Management
- Work Flow Systems
- Knowledge Management

Electronic Information Systems

- Transaction Processing Systems
- Management Information Systems
- Decision Support Systems
- Executive Information Systems
- Expert Systems
- Office Automation Systems

Intranet Technology Resources

- TCP/IP Client/Server Networks
- HTML Web Publishing Software
- Web Browser/Server Suites

Conclusion

Fortunes spring from innovative ideas and the clever use of information. Virtual corporation—a nonpermanent and mobile office—is possible with the growth of computer and communications technology. It will allow managers and employees to spend more time with customers and to improve employee satisfaction and productivity with fewer interruptions. To go ahead, there is no way but to adopt the technology. An early-adopter will have tremendous advantage in this competitive world.

REFERENCES

Sirpolis, "Entrepreneurship and Small Business Management", All India Publishers and Distributors, Chennai, 1998.

Turban, Rainer, Potter, "Introduction to Information Technology", John Wiley & Sons (ASIA) Pte Ltd, Singapore, 2000.

James A. O' Brien, "Management Information Systems", TATA McGraw-Hill Edition, 1999.

Robert Schultheis and Mary Sumner, "Management Information System—The Manager's view", TATA McGraw-Hill Edition, 1999.

Muneesh Kumar, "Business Information Systems", Vikas Publishing Pvt Ltd, 1998.

Information Technology, May 1997, Vol. 6, No. 7, Pg. 81.

Information Technology Sep. 1999, Vol. 8, No. 11, Pg. 16.

Information Technology, April 2000, Vol. 9, No. 6, Pg. 49.

5

Government Assistance and Rural Employment Opportunities

M. Ganesan

Introduction

Rural unemployment and under employment are the factors contributing to the high incidence of poverty in rural areas. Hence creating rural employment has been a major concern of our policy makers. This will ultimately help improve the living conditions of rural poor. Government provides various assistance for rural industrialization. Sectoral incentives and institutional financing are provided for establishing conducive macro environment for rural industries and thereby Government creates employment opportunities in rural areas.

Government Assistance Schemes

A review of and ongoing Government sponsored for rural employment programmes is made under various heads:

1. Integrated Rural Development Programme (IRDP)

The integrated rural development programme was launched in the sixth five year plan in the year 1978-79 in 2000 selected blocks. From October 2, 1980 it was extended to all over the country. The programme was given a powerful thrust in the 8th plan. IRDP is a multi level multi sector and multi section concept of rural development. As a multi concept it encompasses rural development at various levels such as viable cluster of village communities.

2. *Prime Minister's Rozgar Yojna (PMRY)*

It was launched on October 2, 1993 to provide self-employment opportunities to one million educated unemployed youth. The self employment amongst educated unemployed youth would be promoted by setting up seven lakh micro enterprises through industry service and business ventures. The scheme covers both the urban and rural areas.

The scheme covers all educated unemployed youth who are class X passed or failed, ITI passed, and persons who have undergone the Government sponsored technical course for a minimum duration of 6 months. They should be within the age group of 18-35 years. For the purpose of the scheme family income per annum should not exceed Rs. 24000. Upto 1997 6.32 lakh youth have been sanctioned loan.

Projects upto Rs. 1 lakh are covered under the scheme in case of individuals. Banks provide loan upto 95000 and the remaining amount of Rs. 5000 is provided as subsidy by Government.

3. *Employment Assurance Scheme (EAS)*

It is aimed at providing assured employment to all persons in rural areas who are below the poverty line and are seeking employment but to unable to find it. The coverage of EAS has been extended to 3200 blocks. The second stream of Jawahar Rozgar Yojna stands merged with EAS from January 1996. The scope of EAS has been enlarged for taking up horticultural activities of individual land of marginal farmers. Over 4.46 crore persons have been registered under this scheme.

4. *Khadi and Village Industries Commission (KVIC)*

KVIC was established in 1953 with a primary objective of developing Khadi and Village Industries and improving rural employment opportunities. Its wide range of activities include training of Artisans, extension of assistance for procurement of raw materials, marketing of finished products and arrangement for manufacturing and distribution of improved tools, equipment and machinery to producers on concessional terms.

There are about 26 specified village industries such as processing of cereals and pulses, leather, cottage matches, gur, and khandsari, palm gur, non-edible oils and soaps, bee-keeping, village pottery and blacksmithy, gobar gas, household aluminum utensils, etc.

KVIC has identified 26 industries as villages and provides assistance in all its phases of development.

5. District Industrial Centre (DIC)

DICs were established in May 1978 to cater the needs of small units. Each District has a DIC at its headquarters. The prospective small entrepreneur will get all assistance from Government for setting up and running an industrial unit in rural areas.

Functions of DIC are:

- Identification of entrepreneurs
- Selection of projects
- Provisional registration under SSI
- Purchase of fixed assets
- Clearances from various departments
- Assistance to raw material suppliers
- Assistance to village artisans and handicrafts
- Interest free sales tax loan
- Subsidy schemes
- Training programmes
- Self employment for unemployed educated youth

Conclusion

Even though the Government is providing assistance to increase the employment in rural areas, there are still 260 million people below the poverty line. The Government should generate employment opportunities in the fields of agriculture, handlooms, khadi and village industries to which 90 per cent rural works force depends on.

6

Health Cooperative—Need for Manufacturing Generics and Distribution through Cooperative Network

Kibet Leleito Erick

India's population is second to China's population. India has to promote and ensure a healthy population for proper economic development. It is essential to have healthy and strong human resources, working in various sectors of the economy, such as Agriculture, Industry, and Service Sectors.

As per the UNO-Human Development Report, the Health Parameters for India's Health Sector is dismal and showing poor performances. Therefore, there is an urgent need to initiate programmes/projects for strengthening health cooperative sector/system in India. It is heartening to note that, Kerala is one of the leading cooperative health Institutional showcase for providing Medical Health Services to the Society.

They are keen in trying to improve and promote the Health Standards of their population. The involvement of Cooperative System in the Health sector have paved way for better health infrastructure and facilities. The Kerala Co-operative Medical Health Services has catered to the Medical requirements of the society. A large number of cooperative Health centers, clinics, paramedical staff etc., are very helpful to the society community.

These cooperative health institutions are offering full-time employment to the qualified Medical personnel/ Technicians having qualification such as M.B.B.S., Pharmacist, Nurses, Dentists, and other super specialities experts. They are also participating in the cooperative health sector whenever and wherever they are requested to do so.

In Tamilnadu, health cooperative's are weak and not progressing because of numerous management problems and other institutional related constraints. The Snake-Catchers Cooperative Society -(IRULLA-MADRAS) is the single and the only type found in India. It is coming under the purview of Industrial cooperative societies. There is a need to bring it in to health cooperative sector and expand its functions and operations. They can even think of producing medicine and by-products from the "Snake fats" which is very useful for medical purposes. It is the duty of Health Cooperative Society to supply medicine/drugs to its members at a lower cost/price. In this regard, distribution of drugs and medicine can be done through cooperative distributors network. An effective and efficient cooperative network would reduce the distribution cost and improve channel effectiveness in the long run.

The Indian Medical Practitioner and Pharmaceutical Cooperative Store must improve their efficiency by manufacturing generics, specialized drugs/medicines. This type of cooperative institutions would ensure reduction of distribution costs, provide drugs/medicine at cheaper rate/ cost/price, and finally holding the price line.

India is highly endowed and blessed with sufficient medicinal plants such as Neem tree, Cardamom plant, Chicona tree, Honey, Turmeric, Ginger, Suffron etc.

They contain, some of the most important medicinal constituents such as volatile oils etc. The Cardamom

Planters Association for instance, can form cooperatives such as Cardamom Planters Cooperative Health and Pharmaceutical Society to extract this active constituents and provide cheaper drugs and adequate health facilities to its members. To conclude, "a Healthy Society brings Prosperity to the Nation".

7

Challenges to IT Entrepreneurs in India

Haji Dr. M. Sheik Mohamed
D.Sugumar

Introduction

Information Technology is the Industry where through the convergence of computer communication systems and other allied peripherals the rapid spread and dissemination of knowledge and information is achieved. There was a time when IT was regarded as computers but with rapid advancement in an entire array of information delivery systems today IT included within its realm all kinds of media devices used for processing and transmitting information. The sudden advancement of this sector has been universally hailed as a revolution and has made a profound and deep rooted all pervaded impact on human life all over the world. India has not been unaffected by these changes. On the contrary, we have always been in the mainstream of this drama both as the providers of human resources in America and other western countries and also the fastest growing technology sector on our own land.

IT Entrepreneurs

The rapid and visibly outstanding progress in this sector is mainly result of individual entrepreneurship and can easily be quoted as an example of Indian endeavour. Most of the big and successful companies that we have around us owe their existence and sustenance to some remarkable and talented individuals combining in themselves both technical knowhow and acute business acumen. Wipro, Infosys, Satyam, NIIT, HCL and so many other leading companies in IT industry have each of them a few individuals acting as the main propellant.

Contribution of IT Sector

The compound Annual Growth Rate (AGR) in this sector has been more than 50 per cent for the last five years and today it has a turnover of 9.5 billion dollars (Rs. 46000 crores) as against 2 billion dollars (Rs. 9700 crores) in 1994-95. In exports nearly three-fourth of the total turnover of this sector is sent outside the country. Today this sector accounts for 15 per cent of India's total exports standing at dollar 6.5 billion. It is expected that by the year 2008, IT sector will account for an export of dollar 50 billions which shall be roughly 35 per cent of India's total export. Again, as per the Mckinsey Report, by the same year this sector will account for 7.7 percent of India's GDP.

These data are not only impressive, they are also very encouraging. More so, for an economy like ours which is still struggling for finding ways to get out of the category of underdeveloped countries so as to provide the basic minimum to all it is People which will make them capable of leading a life of dignity and comfort.

Going into the details of this sector, we find that the major components of this sector are software and services, hardware, peripherals, training, maintenance and net working of these the software and service subsector is the most important one, not only as being the largest contributor to the overall kitty about also as being primarily export oriented. Its share in the total turnover of this sector is also most two-third. Again more than 25 per cent of it is used in the domestic market. As against this, the hardware sector which comes next in the predominance and size gives nearly 15 per cent of IT revenues. Of this more than 95 per cent is consumed in the domestic market and a meager 5 per cent of it goes for export. Only a very small part of this revenue goes outside the country in the shape of exports and the rest gets used locally.

North America (USA & Canada) account for 62 per cent of our exports followed by Europe where nearly 24 per cent of our export goes. Japan, the rising sun of Asia, accounts for 3.5 per cent of Indian software exports while the South East Asia contributes equally. West Asia, Australia and New Zealand are our other destinations in this regard.

As few as the domestic market is concerned, the central and the various state Governments are the major consumers purchasing nearly one-third of the total interior market consumption. Banking and finance sector account for 18 per cent, manufacturing sector uses 12 per cent and telecom sector uses 10 percent of the domestic IT market.

Today, India boasts of having more than 40 companies that export software worth more than Rs. 100 crores and number of companies exporting software costing more than a crore of rupees goes over 750. This is a spectacular figure and mind boggling. And when we consider the fact that these exports are not being done in traditional goods or primary raw materials, as had often been the case with Indian exports, it becomes even more impressive.

Challenges

The major areas of issues that confront the IT industry include infrastructure and services, electronic governance, education and mass campaign for IT awareness. To provide IT services to the common masses there is an immediate need to have availability and affordability of access devices and the establishment of basic network.

Suggestion and Conclusion

To solve these problems the cost of the access devices needs to be brought down; the cost level of telephone connections needs to be pruned; the cost of installation for internet service providers must be brought to reasonable limits, availability of international bandwidth must be made readily available at reasonable prices and last but not the least, in addition to be use of English language as the medium of interaction, the corresponding regional languages must also be given the required boost.

8

IT—A Money Spinner and Generator of Potential Employment

R. Pandi

Now-a-days Information Technology (IT) is the buzzword. It is gaining momentum in every field. For some, it is a matter of fashion or bringing some convenience both to the buyer and seller, but for the industry as a whole it is a matter of survival. The use of IT and IT enabled services are going to take a spurt over the next one or two years. So, it is the high time to all young entrepreneurs get entered, properly educated, learn about the best and most cost effective options and to log in immediately. IT and IT enabled services are becoming the money spinners and have immense potentiality to generate employment opportunities to millions of educated and talented youths. Hence entrepreneurism in these fields will pay rich dividends.

Business at the speed of light should be the watch word of all young and elite entrepreneurs. It may be a little exaggerated but the world wide developments in this connected field will force the organization to be very fast to acclimatise.

The new millenium has produced a seachange in the thinking of business magnets, entrepreneurs and corporate leaders. Gone are the days where only lip service was enough to satisfy the customers but now the scenario is different. In this digital world, winning the hearts of the people is altogether a different ball game and you need a blue print for avoiding pitfalls in today's volatile consumer driven market.

Europe beckons Indian firms. Why this interest in India, of all countries? Mr. David Muxworthy, Vice-President, Welsh Development Agency says, "The slowdown in the US economy has to be perceived as a serious threat to the growth of Indian IT companies. Europe has a market about the same size as the US and Japan put together. An Indian company setting up base in Wales will have an access to 400 million people and twice that number in a few more years when more countries join the E.U"-[1]. The above statement clearly portrays the potentiality for IT in Europe, and so the young entrepreneurs have to enter into this field which grows at a faster clip than any other field.

Moreover it is time you get recognised for your contribution and innovation in making India a software brand in the global market. The Dewang Mehta Award has been created by the Ministry of Information Technology by Indian government for the first time, will be given every year and it amounts to Rs. 5 Lakhs.

Internet has slowly but surely swept across continents, corporations and homes and created the base for a truly connected world. From just 90,000 Net users in India as recent as in 1997, the number, today has risen to an estimated 30 lakh. Government projections indicate that the number of internet users is slated to touch the 2.5. crore figure within 5 years. In order to facilitate the growth, the government plans to increase the bandwidth capabilities"-[2].

The biggest revolution in the technology has hit the Indian life in recent times and it ensures one thing that the customer can have the last laugh. As far as entrepreneurs are concerned, striking a balanced between making a peaceful living and making a joyful life is becoming harder to pull off in the new technology. So, they have to shoulder the burden of analysing the opportunities and the threats the technology poses. Otherwise, they will be thrown out of this connected world.'

"A study by NASSCOM and Boston consulting group in 2001 indicates that online B2C commerce will reach Rs. 3000 cr by 2005. In companies B2B commerce will reach Rs. 1,92,000 cr in the same year. A recent study by IDC (India) released in October indicates that B2C commerce will grow from Rs. 240 cr. In 2002 to Rs. 2300 cr by 2006"-[3]. This shows that the online portal business is highly dependent on the base of Internet users, which is dependent on the number of Internet connections. So, it is high time for the new entrepreneurs to exploit the situation that will generate both money and employment opportunities to a lot of young people of our country.

The dotcom bust in 2000 and the recession in the US economy have scaled down the spending on IT by most of the companies. Though IT witnessed a slowdown in 2001, it is dynamic and still attracts the best talent in our country. This is going to be the decade for IT enabled services. The growth areas are call centres, Medical Transcription and Data digitisation. Another growth area is business process outsourcing. In the call centre business, gross margins are in the region of 50 per cent. Call centres are concentrated in Delhi and Mumbai. At present, there are more than 400 call centres in India. The NASSCOM an apex body of IT companies in India, points out that there would be more than 10 Lakh IT enabled call centre jobs by 2008. So, the call centre business if properly nurtured will pay high dividends to the entrepreneurs.

Medical Transcription services had, grown albeit in an unorganised manner and in some metros was a lucrative home office operations for many housewives, fetching

Rs. 5000-10,000 a month, 5-6 hours of work in the unsocial hours everyday"-[4]. It is learnt that the Indian Medical Transcription Market is growing at the rate of 20%.

The worldwide BPO market was worth $280 M in 1999 and is expected to touch $ 540 billion by 2004. India's slice of this market is 0.5 though India has advantages like English speaking, talented manpower. Research indicates that the IT enabled services industry created around 36,000 additional jobs in 2002 taking the total employment opportunities to around 1.06 lakh persons as of March 2002. The entrepreneurs should think of Medical transcription and BPO as these seem to be the promising businesses of future.

"IT for all" was the mantra coined in 1998 with a 10 year time span. But halfway there, the legal frame work is still not completed and only a handful of states have seen the benefits trickling down to the average citizen"-[5]. The incomplete legal framework is the major concern. The authorities concerned must look into this problem so that the benefit of technology should penetrate down to the poorest of the poor.

The Ministry of Information Technology was formed in 1999 to give thrust to IT sector and more specifically the software sector. At least 19 states have announced the IT policies and have been attracting investments in the IT sector. The success of these initiatives taken by the governments will be seen only in the coming years.

Finally, the cyber economy in the country will usher in an era of consumer imperialism where industrial houses and entrepreneurs will concentrate on going that extra mile to please the prospective buyer who cares to click at their doorstep. If the Indian Industry wants to survive in IT era, they have to say goodbye to the old brick and mortar system, otherwise they will have to take the back seat of Indian Industry and they can not earn even their cup of tea in the years to come.

References

Business India, Jan 4-17, 2002 p. 97.

Business India, Dec. 24-Jan. 6, 2002 p. 22.

Business India, Nov 11-24, 2002 p. 56.

Anand Parthasarathy, Service with a Cyber Smile, Survey of Indian Industry, 2003, p. 261.

Anand Parthasarathy, Spreading IT too thinly, Survey of Indian Industry, 2003, p. 272.

9

A Study on the Socio-economic Factors Affecting Entrepreneurism in Rural Economy

Dr. N. Namasivayam
Dr. S. Vijayakumar

Introduction

Entrepreneurship is a process comprising several distinct stages. The first stage in the entrepreneurial process is some change in the real world. For example, a war may destroy a country's manufacturing facilities but spare its trained work force as happened in West Germany during the second world war. Such a change leads to changes in every aspect of life in the country. It creates needs for new goods and services. The destruction of Japan's industry during the second world war allowed the country to rebuild its industry from scratch. The second stage in the entrepreneurial process is the idea. For example, microprocessor the brain of personal computer had been in the American market since the early 1970s. A company called Altair had put out a computer that was so personal that one had to put it together oneself. But it was Apple Computers which perceived that computer market was potentially very big.

One may become an entrepreneur in various ways. He may start a new enterprise. Alternatively he may acquire a franchise. In some cases, one may become an entrepreneur by mere accident. However, the decision is largely forced by parents (or) circumstances. For instance, an unemployed person may enter into business because he finds no job. He may use his own savings, family property and credit to start an industry of his own.

Socio-economic Factors Affecting Entrepreneurism

The entrepreneurial activity at any time is dependent upon a complex and varying combination of socio-economic, psychological and other factors. They are:

Caste Origins

To begin with some social groups produce a larger and more capable body of entrepreneurs than other groups. This is due to the influence of prevailing social factors. It has often been suggested that certain religions and castes encourage the growth of entrepreneurial talent, within the country.

The caste system has been found to be exercising its own influence on the occupational mobility. Some religious communities like the Parsees, Marwaris and Sindhees seem to have an affinity for industrial activity. It is true that certain castes have imbibed in themselves a particular culture that fosters entrepreneurship.

Entry into Entrepreneurship

The time and age at which the entry is made into start establishments are important factors. These two factors are considered as an important factor for entrepreneurism. Generally the youngsters are interested to enter into entrepreneurial area because they are ready to accept risk compared to old one.

Family Background

This factor includes size of family, type of family and economic status of family. To some extent, joint family provided family property to invest and expand the family firm. Background of a family in manufacturing provided a source of industrial entrepreneurship.

Religious Background

Religion exercises a strong influence on attitudes towards material gains relatively to efforts. Still certain religion dominates certain type of industries in India because to that extent the particular religion members cooperate with one another while carry out any type of business.

Education and Technical Know-how

Education is one of the significant factors having direct relationship with entrepreneurial developments. As educated persons, they easily differentiate between the useful and useless, the necessary and unnecessary. Besides, education, entrepreneurship and development are interrelated. Education is the best means of developing man's resourcefulness which encompasses different dimensions of entrepreneurship.

Occupational Background

Employed people were more attracted towards entrepreneurship than those engaged in agriculture or business. A sizeable number of entrepreneurs were the unemployed youth prior to starting the industrial units. Entrepreneurship is thus not confined to any particular occupation. What is required is the presence of entrepreneurial spirit and zeal. Most of the entrepreneurs came from families where the parental occupation was agriculture or employment.

Migratory Character

Generally the people will be migrated when the available factors of production are abundant in supply in certain areas. In addition to that, in rural areas most of the favourable atmosphere are not available for the entrepreneur developments.

Type of Industry Started

Depend upon the available resources certain people are interested to start food products, engineering products and cotton business in certain areas, due to availability of various services at cheaper cost.

Type of Ownership Preferred

Generally the people want to establish an enterprise by way of partnership form because the availability of capital and various skills required are limited in rural areas. So they preferred partnership.

Conclusion

Entrepreneurs are not necessarily a special breed. Entrepreneurship is a question of behaviour, policies and practices rather than personality. For example, senior executives in many companies resign from well-paid jobs to launch their own small business. In order to be a successful entrepreneur, what is needed is willingness to learn, to work hard persistently, to exercise self-discipline, to adopt and apply the right policies and practices. An entrepreneurial project requires right relationship, right rewards and right staffing system.

Reference

Gupta, C.B., *Entrepreneurial Development*, Sultan Chand & Sons, New Delhi, 1995.

10

Emerging Emphasis on Medicinal Plants to Motivate Rural Entrepreneurs

A. Oliver Bright

In Tamil Nadu most of the villages are not having sufficient medical facilities. But in all the villages the traditional medicines and treatments are followed to cure all the diseases. The English medicines are not supplied in most of the villages. The Government and Social Service Organizations started providing medical facilities in Tamil Nadu villages but they could not cover all the rural population with adequate facilities. The rural population had to depend on the local doctor called "VAITHYAR". They prepare medicines from the medicinal plants available on the soil. They follow all the traditional method of preparing the medicines, which are based on Homoeopathy, Ayurvedic and Sidda.

Now the people around the globe started realizing the importance of the medicines prepared from the medicinal plants. The urban population concentrates more on homoeopathic, ayurvedic and sidda medicines for treating most of the diseases. They prefer this medicines because it does not have any side effects even in the long run. They feel that these are natural medicines. So the Homoeopathic, Ayurvedic and Sidda medicines are revitalized and the demand for such medicines are boosted with significant care. The medicines used for homoeopathic, ayurvedic and sidda are prepared from medicinal plants, which are naturally available in the soil.

The medicinal plants are found in hedges, waste lands, fields, water logged areas, sacred groves, house gardens, temple gardens, tree branches etc. the seeds, nuts, fruits, flowers, buds, leaves, stems, roots, tubers, barks etc. of the medicinal plants are used directly as medicines. The medicinal plants have different tastes such as sweet, bitter, sour etc. The powder, paste, extract, smoke, ashes, oil and juices are made from the medicinal plants and used as medicines. Such form of medicines are consumed and applied on external physic to cure the diseases.

The medicinal plants do not require any special care to grow. It is easy to cultivate and grow. The Botany department of Scott Christian College prepared a list of cultivable medicinal plants.

The Cultivable medicinal plants with Botanical name and family are given below:

	Botanical Name		*Family*
	1		2
1.	Sesbania grandiflora, Pers.	:	Fabaceae
2.	Glycyrrhiza glabra, Linn.	:	Papilionaceae
3.	Postia strateotes, Linn.	:	Araceae
4.	Euphorbia hirta, Linn.	:	Euphorbiaceae
5.	Withania somnifera, Dun.	:	Solanaceae
6.	Alpinia galanga, Sw.	:	Zingiberanceae
7.	Sida caprinifolia, Linn.	:	Fabaceae
8.	Indigo fera tinctoria, Linn.	:	Fabaceae
9.	Amaranthus tritis, Roxb.	:	Amarataceae
10.	Cynoden dactylon, Pers	:	Poaceae
11.	Adhatoda vasica, Nees.	:	Acanthaceae
12	Aristolochia bracteata, Rets.	;	Aristolochiaceae

	1		2
13.	Capparis horrida, Linn.	:	Capparidaceae
14.	Marsilae quadrifolia, Linn.	:	Marsileaceae
15.	Fiscus bengalensis, Linn.	:	Moraceae
16.	Cassia auriculata, Linn.	:	Caesalpiniaceae
17.	Citrullus colocynthes, Schrader.	:	Cucurbitaceae
18.	Zinginer officinale, Rose.	:	Zingiberaceae
19.	Bassia longifolia, J. Koenig.	:	Sapotaceae
20.	Aristolochia indica, Linn.	:	Aristolochiaceae
21.	Odina wodier, Roxb.	:	Anacardiaceae
22.	Dtura metel, Linn.	:	Solanaceae
23.	Calotropis gigantea, R. Br.	:	Asclepladaceae
24.	Ipomoea reniformis, Chois.	:	Convolvulaceae
25.	Coleus aromaticus, Benth.	:	Lamiaceae
26.	Ionidium suffruitcosum, Ging.	:	Viloaceae
27.	Ocimum Canum, Sims.	:	Lamiaceae
28.	Terminalia chebula, Retz.	:	Combretacea
29.	Solanum surattense, Burm, F	:	Solanaceae
30.	Eclipta alba, Hassk.	:	Asteraceae
31.	Erythrina incica, Linn.	:	Fabaceae
32.	Tricodesma indicus, R. Br.	:	Boraginaceae
33.	Carrisa carandus, Linn.	:	Apcyabaceae
34.	Solanum xanthocarpum, S&W.	:	Solanaceae
35.	Murraya koenigii Spreng (Bergera Koenigii)	:	Rutlaceae
36.	Clitoria ternatea, Linn.	:	Fabaceae
37.	Jatropha curcas, Lonn.	:	Euphorbiaceae
38.	Canthium parviflorum, Lam.	:	Rubiaceae
39.	Phyllanthus niruri, Linn.	:	Euphorbiaceae
40.	Acalypha indica, Linn.	:	Euphorbiaceae
41.	Aloe vera, Linn.	:	Lillaceae
42.	Sphaeranthus indicus, Linn.	:	Compositae
43.	Plumbago zeylanacis, Linn.	:	Plumbaginaceae
44.	Psidium guajava, L.	:	Myrtaceae
45.	Andrographis echoides, Nees.	:	Acanthaceae

1		2
46. Cyperus rotundus, Linn.	:	Cyperaceae
47. Cocinia indica, W&A	:	Cucurbitaceae
48. Polycarpeae corymbosa, Lam.	:	Caryophyllaceae
49. Trianthoma decandra, Linn.	:	Aizoaceae
50. Santalum album, Linn.	:	Santalaceae
51. Cassia fistula, Linn.	:	Caesalpiniaceae
52. Trianthima portulacastrun, Linn.	:	Aizoaceae
53. Asystasia gangetica, S.	:	Acanthaceae
54. Indigofera aspalathoides, Vahl.	:	Papillionaceae
55. Amaranthus polygamus, Linn.	:	Amaranthaceae
56. Heliotropium indicum, Linn.	:	Boaragineacea
57. Tinospora cardifolia, Meirs.	:	Menispermaceae
58. Solanum tervam, Linn.	:	Solanaceae
59. Hibiscus Rosa-sinensis, Linn.	:	Malvaceae
60. Clerodendron phlomoides, Linn.	:	Verbenaceae
61. Terminalia bellirica (Gaetrner) Roxb.	:	Combretaceae
62. Piper longum, Linn.	:	Piperaceae
63. Ocimum basillicum, Linn.	:	Lamiaceae
64. Abutilon indicum, G. Don.	:	Malvaceae
65. Lucas aspera, Spreng.	:	Lamiaceae
66. Ocimum sanctum, Linn.	:	Lamiaceae
67. Solanum trillobatum, Linn.	:	Solanaceae
68. Cocos nucifera, Linn.	:	Arecaceae
69. Tylophora asthmatica, W&A.	:	Asclepiadeceae
70. Spermacoce hispida, Linn.	:	Rubiaceae
71. Ervatamia coronaria, Stapf.	:	Apocyanaceae
72. Gynandropis pentaphylla, D.C.	:	Caparidaceae
73. Hemidesmus indicusm, R. Br.	:	Asclepiadaceae
74. Achyranthus aspera, Linn.	:	Amarantaceae
75. Syzygium jambolanum, D.C.	:	Myrtaceae
76. Catheranthus roseos, (L) G.Dun.	:	Apocyanaceae
77. Cassia obtusa, W&A.	:	Caesalpiniaceae
78. Andrographis paniculata, Nees.	:	Acanthaceae

1		2
79. Asteracantha longifolia, Nees.	:	Acanthaceae
80. Morinda tinctoria, Roxb.	:	Rubiaceae
81. Tribulus terretris, Linn.	:	Zygophyllaceae
82. Phyllanthus emblica, Linn.	:	Euphorbiaceae
83. Vitex negundo, Lin.	:	Verbanaceae
84. Carica papaya, Linn.	:	Caricaceae
85. Mollugo ceerviana, Ser.	:	Aizoaceae
86. Sida cardifolia, Linn.	:	Cucurbitaceae
87. Momordica charantia, Linn.	:	Cucurbitaceae
88. Optuntia dillenii, Haw.	:	Cactaceae
89. Pavetta indica, Linn.	:	Rubiaceae
90. Cissus quadrangularis, Linn.	:	Vitaceae
91. Argemone mexicana, L.	:	Papavaranceae
92. Moniera cuneifolia, Michx.	:	Scrophulariaceae
93. Streblus asper, Lour.	:	Moraceae
94. Clerodentron inerme, Gaertn.	:	Verbenaceae
95. Anisomeles malabarica, R. Br.	:	Lamiaceae
96. Lippia nodiflora, Mich.	:	Verbenaceae
97. Altermanthera sessilis (L), R. Br. ExDC.	:	Amaranthaceae
98. Cassia senna, Linn.	:	Caesalpiniaceae
99. Lawsonia inermis, Linn.	:	Lythraceas
100. Punica granatum Linn.	:	Punicaeae
101. Crataeva religiosa, Forst.	:	Capparidiaceae
102. Toddalia asiatica, Lam.	:	Rulaceae
103. Tapsicum frutescens, Linn.	:	Solanaceae
104. Croton sparsiflorus, Morong.	:	Euphorbiaceae
105. Piper nugrum, Linn.	:	Piperaceae
106. Mukia maderaspatana (L) M. Roemer.	:	Cucurbitaceae
107. Cardiospermum halicacabum Lin.	:	Sapindaceae
108. Merrimia tridendata, Hallier.	:	Convolvulaceae
109. Cardiospermum halicacabum Lin.	:	Moringaceae
110. Amaranthus spinosus, Linn.	:	Amaranthaceae
111. Boerhaavia diffusa, Linn.	:	Nyctaginaceae

	1		2
112.	Acorus calamus, Linn.	:	Aroidaceae
113.	Centella asiatica, Urb.	:	Apiaceae
114.	Deloniz elata, Gamble, n. Comb.	:	Caesalpiniaceae
115.	Musa paradisiaca, Linn.	:	Musaceae
116.	Dichrostachys cinerea, W&A.	:	Mimosaceae
117.	Hymenodictyon exceksum, Wall.	:	Rubiaceae
118.	Aegle marmelos, Corr.	:	Rutaceae
119.	Evolvulus alsinoides, Linn.	:	Convolvulaceae
120.	Enicostemma, littorale, B1.	:	Gentianaceae
121.	Azadirachta indica, A. Juss.	:	Meliaceae
122.	Daemia extensa, R.Br.	:	Asclepiadaceae
123.	Cannabis	:	Sativa

Applications of Medicinal Plants

The medicinal plants are processed into consumable form such as powder, paste, extract, smoke, ashes, oil and juice for curing different diseases. It prevents and cures most of the diseases of human beings and animals. These are applied to cure and prevent biles, sinus, mucus, cough, rheumatism, body pain, fever, throat pain, tonsils, piles, tooth ache, stomach pain, hiccuff, leucoderma, toxins, jaundice, rashes, dandruff, diabetics, ulcer, vomit, mouth ulcer, insect bites, dog bite, snake bites, neck pain, snore, acidity, dysentery, arthritis and other diseases of human beings and animals. (Collected from *"Meteria Medica"*).

The medicinal plants are required in tons to prepare medicines for multinational companies like to produce medicines, tablets, oil, soaps, paste, lotion, juice, syrup, extracts etc. made out of herbs.

1. Dabur
2. Medimix
3. Hindustan Lever
4. Tata Pharmaceutical plants
5. Colgate Palmolive,

Even though the medicinal plants have wider applications and demands, the growers are not encouraged. Tamil Nadu soil has good potentials for growing most of the medicinal plants. The growers feel that it is not a yielding sector. The *'vaithyars'* (manufacturers) feel very difficult to market such medicines. The following are the problems identified out of survey made on 100 (One Hundred) *'vaithyars'* in Tamil Nadu.

1. Non-availability of fresh medicinal plants in the soil (They quoted some medicinal plants, green leaves and fresh nuts, flowers, buds, roots etc. to prepare the medicines).
2. Absolutely no growers and even destroyed by animals and human beings without any care.
3. No financial assistance to cultivate and produce such medicinal plants.
4. No marketing facilities such as
   (i) Distribution Network
   (ii) Standardisation
   (iii) Customer relation and feed back
   (iv) Advertising network to intimate and educate
5. Adulteration in quality (It is quoted that some chemicals are used to make the oil and extracts more greenish).
6. No facilities to preserve seasonal medicinal plants which cannot be dried and preserved. (Certain medicines require only fresh plants)
7. No facilities for research and development.

Problems identified from a survey made from 500 customers using Homoeopathic, ayurvedic and sidda medicines in Chennai.

1. Non-availability of medicine in all medical stores.
2. Fear of quality and adulteration in locally prepared medicines.

3. No standardisation.
4. Lack of knowledge in using it.

Findings

1. It is found that this sector is completely unorganized even though many people (*vaithyars*) are involved in preparing and marketing the medicines processed from medicinal plants.
2. Growers are not available because there is no institution encouraging the village people to grow by providing financial assistance, collection, distribution and preservation.
3. No institution or agency to standardize and grade such medicines.
4. Non-availability of efficient distribution network.
5. Non-availability of medium to intimate and educate. (It was quoted that some medicines like oil and extracts require knowledge of method of using it)
6. Many plants like Cannabis sativa are used for preparing indoxicated drinks.

Recommendations

1. The local manufacturers are not formally organized under an institution. So an institution must be set up to organize the local producers (*vaithyars*) to get official affiliation. Such institution must take care of the standardization and grading of medicines appearing in market in the form of oil, extracts, powder, ashes, juice, tablets, paste, soap, cream, lotion, syrup etc. processed from different parts of medicinal plans. Such institution must prevent the adulteration and malpractice and gradation must be made to ensure the customers about their quality.
2. Financial assistance must be provided by/through co-operative banks and rural development banks. It must also provide necessary infrastructure to

preserve the dried and fresh medicinal plants, which are seasonal in nature.

3. The Government institutions shall come forward to make arrangements with multination companies for collection of such materials, price fixation, settlement etc. A fair price must be paid to the growers considering their strain, risk, cost and other social concerns. A steady and regular market for their produce must assured.
4. The Government may provide some lands and employ growers to produce the medicinal plants and local people (*vaithyars*) may be appointed to process it.
5. In order to intimate and educate the values of using the herbal products and the method of using them must be sponsored by Government agencies through radio and televisions.
6. A Society can be formed to take care of this sector (Financial assistance, Collection, Cultivation, Distribution Network etc.)

Marketing Network

1. ABCD Chain Network (Distribution Chain Management)

The Malaysian Tamil Doctor E. Maheswaran started a herbal food marketing company in 1986 in the name Rohini Herbal Products. They introduced their products in Chennai in the name Runi Herbals. They introduced a marketing technique to market their product called "ABCD level Distribution System". It is a multi level marketing network under which there are four levels of customers. They will appoint a group of distributors called Customer A, the Customer A will introduce the next segment called Customer B, the B segment will introduce the next segment called Customer C. The C segment of customers will introduce the next segment called Customer D. Such chain of distribution network is called "ABCD level" chain. Here the A segment will get 15% margin, B segment 6%,

C segment 3% and D segment 2%. In addition to this they have appointed Direct Stockist and C&F agents.

2. BUZZ *Marketing and Retail Network (Supply Chain Management)*

Emmanuel Rosen in his book "The Anatomy of Buzz" uses the compact term "BUZZ" which he defines as "the aggregate of all persons to person communication about a particular product, service or company at any point in time". The "BUZZ" includes

(a)	In store events	-	Each visit of the customer must ensure that he experiences a new aspect of store experience.
(b)	An element of surprise	-	The customers must encounter with different product, services or offer during his visits.
(c)	Bargain create Buzz	-	Certain allowances create buzz but it should not degrade the image of the store/outlet.
(d)	Human experiences beyond the expectations	-	It creates buss when the customers experience more than their expectations in the retail outlet.

As most of the Indian customers are influenced by "BUZZ" group. This strategy of supply chain management can be adopted successfully for marketing the herbal products. The supply chain management must properly designed. In cities and towns many stores must be made with good chain of supply management.

3. *Customer Relationship Management (CRM)*

If we do not realize the needs and practices of the customers the true potentials cannot be identified and visualized. CRM demands that we must go beyond the transaction view of the customers and take a life time view of our relationship with them. The Indian retail outlets must have the relevant data of the customers. This is highly suitable for Herbal marketing network. The retail outlets must keep the relevant data to access the true potential market of each product.

Scope for Growth

The use of chemical substances in food and medical products proved lot of side effects and ill health in the short run and long run. Many costume, hotel, beauty care, food, health care product industries use the chemicals and artificial flavour in production. Even though it gives immediate satisfaction it cause injuries to health. So the people started realizing the need for natural medicines. They are manufactured from the medicinal plants, which are the gifts of nature. It is proved that they do not have harm and side effects even in long run. Many people started using it even in urban areas. So it has wider scope in foodstuffs, clinical field, hospitality industries, hygienic products, beauty clinics, health care products etc. more over the surgery is not recommended in Ayurvedic and sidda treatments, which the people like the most.

Many researches are conducted in the field to find out the applications in different areas. One of the latest researches made by National Institute of Communicative Diseases, New Delhi, found that cannabis oil made from cannabis sativa kills the mosquito larvae. So this natural oil will not cause any harm to health of human being and animals. (Ref. Science Express 29.12.1998). Excellent treatments are available for dog bite, snakebite, jaundice, stroke, phileria etc in villages. The medicines are prepared from the medicinal plants. These were unemphasised but revitalised after realizing their importance.

References

Meteria Medica., A famous book for Ayurvedic and Sidda Medicines.

Medicinal Plants., By Chopra.

A&M Business Magazine.

Indian Management Journal.

Science Express., Supplement of Indian Express.

Valar Thozhil., Tamil Magazine.

11

Entrepreneurs and Stress

(A study with reference to small scale entrepreneurs in Pondicherry)

Prof. A. Viswanathan

Introduction

In an enterprise, land, labour and capital are separately owned respectively by land owners, labourers and financiers and are divorced from one another. It is the entrepreneur's organising ability which brings them together in proper proportions at reasonable rates and harnesses them to work in production, so as to yield the best returns. As an organiser, he guarantees the specific seems to landlords, labourers and financiers in return for assignments made to them. Thus, the entrepreneur is subject to large element of risk. He starts the enterprise, organises it, supervises it and engineers long-run plans of the enterprise.

Economic development essentially means a process of upward change whereby the real per capita income of a country increases over a long period of time. The crucial role displayed by the entrepreneurs in the development of the western countries has made the people of underdeveloped countries too much conscious of the significance of entrepreneurship for economic development.

The entrepreneurs contribute more in the Economy with relatively more favourable opportunity conditions than in the Economy with relatively less favourable opportunity conditions. The establishment of Entrepreneurship Development Institutes and alike by the Indian Government during the last decade is a god testimony to her strong realisation about the *Premier Mobile* role of entrepreneurship played in economic development.

Objectives and Methodology

This study has been attempted to ascertain the socio-economic background of entrepreneurs in and around Pondicherry and their incentives, facilities, infrastructural support and the stress encountered by them in achieving their final objective.

The present study was an attempt based on the following objectives:

1. To identify the general stressors in the entrepreneurs business life.
2. To find out the motivating factors for entrepreneurs to take up to small scale business.
3. To analyse the procedural, promotional, and operational stress factors of the entrepreneurs.

The study is with special reference to small scale units and entrepreneurs in the industrial estates situated around Pondicherry town. Totally 85 entrepreneurs were taken for the study.

Primary data and Secondary data were collected through a questionnaire and from the data available from the Department of Industries, Pondicherry respectively.

Analysis

Respondents-Age-wise

The analysis reveals that the age has a direct impact on stress factors. The experienced and aged entrepreneurs will be able to absorb stress factors much more easily than the young entrepreneurs. On the other hand young and inexperienced entrepreneurs will get a jolt whenever they are forced to face certain problems leading to stress.

Table 11.1 Distribution of Respondents Age-wise

Age class interval	*No. of Respondents*	*Percentage*
21-25	4	4.7
26-30	12	14.1
31-35	18	21.2
36-40	21	24.7
41 45	13	15.3
46-50	12	14.1
51-55	2	2.4
56-60	2	2.4
61-65	1	1.1
Total	**85**	**100.00**

Source: Primary Data.

Table 11.1 shows the age classification of entrepreneur's majority (24.7%) of the entrepreneurs are between the age group of 36 to 40. This is followed by the age group between 31 to 35 (21.27%). 5.9% of entrepreneurs, are above the age of 50 years, it is worth mentioning that among the total respondents, 68 respondents are below the age of 45. It is therefore understandably assumed that respondent's response will add to the strength of the study.

Respondents—Community-wise

The entrepreneurs of the sample too confirm to the established theorem. Table 11.2 shows that out of 85 entrepreneurs contacted 18.8% belonged to the trading community, followed by the farmers (15.3%) who have also taken up the industrial activities, particularly because of the increasing pressure on land and the industrial incentives available to them. It is interesting to note that 45.9% of the entrepreneurs are not falling in any of the first four categories given in Table 11.2.

Table 11.2: Distribution of Respondents Community-wise

Sl. No.	*Communities*	*Number of Respondents*	*Percentage*
1.	Brahmins	9	10.6
2.	Traders	16	18.8
3.	Landlords	8	9.4
4.	Framers	13	15.3
5.	Others	39	45.9
	Total	**85**	**100.00**

Source: Primary Data.

Respondents—Religion-wise

The religion-wise distribution of the sample respondents proves that the entrepreneurial activities of cross-section of the society are also affected by the religious following of its milieu. It is also noteworthy that the domination of a particular religion in an area largely influences these statistics. Hence, it should be viewed in this particular perspective. Table 11.3 shows that the Hindus (94.1%) dominate the scene, followed by Christians (5.9%).

Table 11.3: Distribution of Respondents Religion-wise

Sl. No.	*Religion*	*Number of Respondents*	*Percentage*
1.	Hindus	80	94.1
2.	Christians	5	5.9
	Total	**85**	**100.00**

Source: Primary Data.

Respondents—Economic and Technical Background

The economic and technical background of the entrepreneurs also proves that persons with technically qualified takes up the entrepreneurial activities. Table 11.4 indicates that persons with technical background lead in entrepreneurial activities (37.6%) followed by the family business background (27.1%). It is interesting to note that white collar takes up the least position among the sample respondents.

Table 11.4: Distribution of Respondents Economic and Technical Background-wise

Sl. No.	*Background*	*No. of Respondents*	*Percentage*
1.	Family Business	23	27.1
2.	Technically Qualified	32	37.6
3.	Origin from working class	18	21.2
4.	Origin from White Collar	5	5.9
5.	Others	7	8.2
	Total	**85**	**100.00**

Source: Primary Data.

Motivational Drive

The analysis proves the thinking that people from the particular socio-economic background, the technically qualified seem to prefer the industrial ventures in large numbers in Pondicherry. However, the tilt of family business towards the entrepreneurial activities is an interesting phenomenon.

Table 11.5 shows the major motivational cause for an entrepreneur to start a small scale Industry.

In the ranking position of the Respondents, earning profits occupy the first place (24.31%). All the persons want to survive in the competitive markets. Without money they cannot live. For them, profit is the only way to make money. For instance, after investing a lot of money into the business and without any outcome may result in disappointment. So, the respondents are of the opinion that earning profit is a major motivating factor.

It is always wrong to tell that entrepreneurs are only for profit and money making. Especially in the present

Table 11.5: Cause of Motivational Drive

Sl. No.	Major causes	Entrepreneurs Ranking No:1	No:2	No:3	Weighted Score	Rating (Percent)	Rank
1.	Unemployment	8	5	2	36	7.06	VII
2.	Dissatisfaction of previous job	8	9	9	51	10.00	VI
3.	To Make use of Financial Assistance from Pondicherry government	12	15	13	79	15.49	III
4.	To Produce the best Product	17	8	18	85	16.67	II
5.	To Earn more Profit	19	25	17	124	24.31	I
6.	To give Employment	5	11	17	54	10.59	V
7.	To Achieve Some Meritorious Service to the Society	14	12	8	74	14.51	IV
8.	Any other Reason	2	-	1	7	1.37	VIII
	Total	**85**	**85**	**85**	**510**	**100.00**	

Source: Primary Data.

context of consumer awareness in India, there are several other ideas and visions for which persons take the business venture. Table 11.6 portray an insight into these aspects of their roles.

Table 11.6: Entrepreneurial Vision of the Respondents

Sl. No.	Entrepreneurial Vision	Number of Respondents	Percentage
1.	Status Consciousness	18	21.2
2.	Wealth Consciousness	30	35.3
3.	Service Consciousness	35	41.2
4.	Others	2	2.3
	Total	85	**100.00**

Source: Primary Data.

An analysis of the intricate socio-economic aspects of one's vision before entering into the area of entrepreneurship reveals that service consciousness (41.2%) assumes the top place followed by the wealth consciousness (35.3%).

Table 11.7: General Stress Factors in the Entrepreneur's Life

Sl. No.	*Nature of Stress*	*Entrepreneurs Ranking*			*Weighted Score*	*Rating (Percent)*	*Rank*
		No:1	*No:2*	*No:3*			
1.	Financial Risk/loss	12	7	6	56	10.98	IV
2.	Technical/Machinery	4	16	26	70	13.73	III
3.	Marketing/competitors	49	18	9	192	37.65	I
4.	Labour/Attitude of Labour	10	23	17	93	18.23	II
5.	Communicational	2	3	6	18	3.53	VI
6.	Private Life	2	2	3	13	2.55	VIII
7.	Transport	5	13	10	51	10.00	V
8.	Local Legal Situations	1	3	6	15	2.94	VII
9.	Any other Factor	-	-	2	2	0.39	IX
	Total	**85**	**85**	**85**	**510**	**100.00**	

Source: Primary Data.

Table 11.7 shows the general stress factors in the entrepreneur's life. In the entrepreneur's ranking, competitors and marketing occupies the first position. (37.65%) competition plays an important role in business. Because of the advertisement cost the entrepreneur has to face many more marketing problems.

Table 11.8: Procedural Stress Factors faced by Entrepreneurs

Sl. No.	*Nature of Stress*	*Entrepreneurs Ranking*			*Weighted Score*	*Rating (Per cent)*	*Rank*
		No:1	*No:2*	*No:3*			
1.	Arrangement of Finance	30	27	21	165	32.35	I
2.	Obtaining Licence	27	22	18	143	28.04	II
3.	Government Rules and Regulations	10	14	17	75	14.71	IV
4.	Arranging for Sheds	12	13	16	78	15.29	III
5.	Others	6	9	13	49	9.61	V
	Total	**85**	**85**	**85**	**510**	**100.00**	

Source: Primary Data.

Table 11.8 shows the Procedural Stress Factors faced by the Entrepreneurs. From their opinion finance is the main issue and acts as the major procedural stress factor (32.35%). Because only 22% of the required fund was sanctioned by the Government, banks and financial institutions, finance proved to be a major stress factor.

Table 11.9: Promotional Stress Factors faced by Entrepreneurs

Sl. No.	*Nature of Stress*	*Entrepreneurs Ranking*			*Weighted Score*	*Rating (Per cent)*	*Rank*
		No:1	*No:2*	*No:3*			
1.	Competition/Marketing	38	29	13	185	36.27	I
2.	Raw Material	22	33	20	152	29.80	II
3.	Transportation	11	16	29	94	18.43	III
4.	Shortage of Skilled Laboures	9	5	15	52	10.20	IV
5.	Others	5	2	8	27	5.30	V
	Total	**85**	**85**	**85**	**510**	**100.00**	

Source: Primary Data.

Table 11.9 shows the Promotional Stress Factors faced by the entrepreneurs. Stiff competition and cut-throat marketing is considered to be the major stress factor among the promotional stress factors faced by entrepreneurs. In every business there will be competition, because it is a competitive world. In the competition, marketing plays a vital role. While marketing the goods, the entrepreneur has to advertise. It will increase the expenditure and this cannot be easily adjusted by the small-scale entrepreneurs. He also has to face the problems created by the middlemen.

Table 11.10 shows the various Operational Stress Factors. Machinery is the major factor which leads to stress. Due to frequent power cut, and improper use of machinery stress arises. If the technicians are nearby, the problem can be rectified quickly. But if the technicians are not available, they have to forgo production for some days. This will be a very difficult task for the small scale entrepreneurs.

Table 11.10: Operational Stress Factors faced by Entrepreneurs

Sl. No.	*Nature of Stress*	*Entrepreneurs Ranking*			*Weighted Score*	*Rating (Per cent)*	*Rank*
		No:1	*No:2*	*No:3*			
1.	Labor	30	29	23	171	33.53	II
2.	Power	14	24	31	121	23.73	III
3.	Machinery	39	27	17	188	36.86	I
4.	Others	2	5	14	30	5.88	IV
	Total	**85**	**85**	**85**	**510**	**100.00**	

Source: Primary Data.

Entrepreneurship in this area is still caste-based which evinced by an overwhelming majority of the Hindu castes (94.1%) in the total respondents. The other caste, viz., the Christians (5.9%) are poorly represented. The Muslims, Jains and others are, however, totally underrepresented in the present sample.

Findings and Conclusions

From the view of the Respondents, vision Service consciousness occupies the first place (41.2%). Profit is also a main cause for staring the industry, at the same time they are eager to do some service also to the society. From the General stress factors in the Entrepreneur's life it is inferred that marketing of their products and competition from other producers place first.

Arrangement of Finance occupies the first place in the procedural stress factors faced by entrepreneurs. It's rating percentage is 32.35. Again Marketing/Competition occupies the first rank in the promotional stress factors faced by Entrepreneurs. Its rating percentage is 36.27. In the operational stress factors faced by Entrepreneurs, Machinery problems occupy the first in the respondents point of view. It's rating percentage is 36.86.

This study has brought out a definite view that stress factors have been acting on the life of entrepreneurs in

Pondicherry. There have been certain stress factors which are not outcome of the study. This reveals that Entrepreneurs in general are better placed in Pondicherry in comparison with the entrepreneurs of South Arcot District or near by Districts. It may be due to the excellent effort of measures taken by the Department of Industries, Pondicherry in particular and the Government of Pondicherry in general.

12

Rural Employment Opportunities and Policy Initiatives

J. Madhi Vani

Introduction

India is predominantly a *"rural country"*. Over 74% of population of India lives in rural area. A majority of them, nearly 80%, are engaged in agriculture. As a result of growth of economy, the share of agricultural employment is expected to be 60% in 2000-2001, whereas the rural work force is growing at 1.8% per annum. This vast manpower resource has, in its fold, the poorest of the rural poor. But the strength of this segment of population is:

- Large and growing potential workers,
- Abundant resources of raw material,
- Traditional skills and capacity for initiation of viable small enterprises and
- Large and increasing demand for goods and services.

This would provide the way for employment generation, especially in the non-agro sector.

Generating rural employment in developing countries is essentially an attempt to improve the living conditions of the rural poor. During the early 1960s development policies in the third world centered on growth maximization with in the frame work of modernization approach. Rural employment is a strategy designed to improve the economic and social life of a specific group of rural people living below the poverty line. It involves extending the benefits of development to the poorest among those who seek a livelihood in the rural areas and the group includes small-scale farmers, tenants and the landless labours.

Employment Opportunities in Rural Area

Some of the rural employment opportunities are as follows:

(i) Poultry

(ii) Dairy unit

(iii) Mini rice or wheat mill

(iv) Leather and animal waste based industries

(v) Brick molding

(vi) Floral crafts

(vii) Brass metal crafts

(viii) Handlooms

(ix) Plastic slates

(x) Dustless chalk

(xi) Hand made paper rope and

(xii) Other handicrafts etc.

Government Assistance for Rural Employment

The government's programmes mainly of two kinds. The first one seeks to promote self employment by providing the poor households with productive assets, financed by subsidies and credit. The other seeks to provide wage employment and in the process creates community assets.

Some of the government assisted programmes are as follows:

Employment Assurance Scheme(EAS):

Employment Assurance Scheme (EAS) was launched on 2nd October 1993. This scheme is a centrally sponsored scheme on cost sharing basis between the centre and the states in the ratio of 75:25. The primary objective of Employment Assurance Scheme (EAS) is to provide assured employment of 100 days of unskilled manual work to the rural poor who are in need of employment and seek it.

Jawahar Gram Samridhi Yojana (JGSY)

Jawahar Gram Samridhi Yojana (JGSY) is with effect from 1st April 1999. The cost sharing ratio between the centre and the states is also 75:25. The primary objective of this scheme is to enable the rural poor to increase the opportunities for sustained employment. The secondary objective is to generate supplementary employment for the unemployed in rural areas.

Swarnajayanti Gram Swarozgar Yojana (SGSY)

Swarnajayanti Gram Swarozgar Yojana (SGSY) was launched with effect from April 1st, 1999. Financing of the programmes is shared between the centre and the state in the ratio of 75:25. The objective under the scheme is to bring every assisted family above the poverty line in three years. It also aims at establishing large number of micro enterprise.

Prime Minister's Rozgar Yojana (PMRY)

Prime Minister's Rozgar Yojana (PMRY) is for self-employment. Unemployed youth are still not in a position its under take projects involving investment. To sort it out, the Prime Minister's Rozgar Yojana is an ideal and dynamic channel for generating jobs to the job seekers though self-employment. The scheme was formally announced by Prime Minister of 15th August, 1993 and launched on 2nd, October, 1993.

Micro Finance for Micro Enterprises

Micro finance is provided for establishing micro enterprises by rural entrepreneurs. Micro enterprises have emerged as a real boon for the poor. Development of micro enterprises helps to create immediate employment opportunities to people of low investment level. Special emphasis will be placed on promotion of micro enterprises in rural area as set up by vulnerable sections, including women, scheduled castes, scheduled tribes and other backward classes.

Micro enterprise is defined in terms of investment up to Rs. 1 lakh in plant and machinery. As per the Annual Survey of Industries (ASI) 1992-93 micro enterprises accounted for 23% of the total Registered industrial units with the largest employment consisting 11% of the total industrial labour force.

Integrated Rural Development Programme (IRDP)

Integrated Rural Development Programme (IRDP) aims at providing self employment to the rural poor through acquisitions of productive assets which would generate additional income on a sustained basis to enable them to cross the poverty line. Assistance is provided in the form of subsidy and bank credit. There is mandatory quota to choice the beneficiaries from scheduled castes, scheduled tribes and women. The scheme is in operation since 1980.

Training of Youth for Self Employment (TRYSEM)

Training of Youth for Self Employment (TRYSEM) is a facilitating component of IRDP (Integrated Rural Development Programme), providing basic technical and entrepreneurial skills to the rural poor in the age groups of 18 to 35 years to take up income generating activities after undergoing professional training in various fields in the established and recognized training institutes.

Development of Women and Children in Rural Areas (DWCRA)

Development of Women and Children in Rural Areas (DWCRA) was initiated in 1982-83 for strengthening the "gender" components of IRDP (Integrated Rural Development Programme). It is directed at improving standard of living of women through the provision of opportunities for self employment through skill up-gradation, training, credit and other support services.

Small Industries Development Organisation (SIDO)

Small Industries Development Organisation (SIDO) acts as a policy formulating, coordinating and monitoring agency for the development of small scale industries at national level.

National Small Industries Corporation (NSIC)

National Small Industries Corporation (NSIC) was established in 1955 with the view to assist, promote, develop and finance small scale industries in the country.

(i) To secure government orders for the small industries

(ii) To provide loans

(iii) To provide technical assistance

(iv) To secure coordination between small scale and large scale industries, so that the former produce goods required by the latter.

Entrepreneurship Development Programmes (EDPs)

Entrepreneurship Development Programmes (EDPs) play a crucial role in the formation and development of entrepreneurial personality. Motivational training is provided during the EDPs to help trainees develop such a personality. Counseling is considered as an important method to help participant select appropriate business opportunities, prepare business places and for effective implementation of the project and management of an enterprise.

District Industries Centers (DICs)

The District Industries Centers (DICs) programme was launched in 1978 throughout the country to help in effective development of small tiny and college industries all over the country including, rural and back was areas with greater emphasis on maximum generation of employment.

Other Government Policy Measures

Government's policy initiatives in recent times have improved the policy environment. The statement on industrial policy announced on 24th July 1991 and the policy measures for promoting and strengthening small tiny and cottage enterprises announced on 6th August 1991 have set the tone of new era of small scale industries development. They are as follows:

- Procedures to be followed by small scale industries have been simplified, bureaucratic controls effectively reduced and unnecessary interference have been eliminated to enable the entrepreneurs to concentrate on production and marketing functions.
- Steps have been taken by the government to ensure adequate and equitable distribution of indigenous and imported raw materials. The policies have been designed in such a way that, they do not militate against entry of new units. Based on the capacity needs, tiny, small scale units are being given priority in allocation of indigenous raw materials.
- A Technology Development Cell (TDC) has been set up in the Small Industries Organisation (SIDO), which provide technology inputs to improve productivity and competitiveness of the products of the small scale sector.

Conclusion

The challenge of new century is to protect and develop villages. To protect villages, a rural employment is necessary.

To sum up rural employment is a weapon to fight against poverty but when it is clubbed with the government and people's participation it becomes the powerful weapon to fight rural poverty.

13

Impact of WTO on Rural Small Entrepreneur in India

Dr. V. Selvaraj

The Importance of dairy in the Indian Economy can be gauged from the fact that milk is the single largest item, which is estimated to fetch Rs. 450 billion way ahead of rice and wheat. The estimated value of the animals alone is around Rs. 35 billion. Dairy animals also contribute to hides/Skins and dung valued at Rs. 60 billion. Dairy sector provides additional income and generates job opportunities for 80 million farmer families. More than 70% of marginal farmers and landless labour maintain dairy animals to supplement their income. Women contribute 71% of the labour force to dairy as compared their share of 33% in crop farming. India now stands number one in milk production in the world. There are more than 97,000 milk co-operative societies in 264 districts as per *AMUL* pattern and at present this sector grows at the rate of 6.5% per annum. Millions of entrepreneur is doing dairy as business. With the advent of liberalisation and move towards globalisation, Indian economic environment offers challenge to entrepreneurs, who is involving in dairy industry.

Dairy is one of the sectors affected by WTO. During the negotiations in 1985, we failed to bargain and agree to allow import of milk and milk products under zero per cent bound duty. In 1999, Indian traders imported 10,000 metric tones of milk powder and in 2000, we were threatened by the arrival of fresh milk in Mumbai from New Zealand at the landed cost Rs. 9. Fortunately, the Govt. of India in it's budget of 2001 has imposed heavy duty on milk and the problem has been halted temporarily. This duty will have to be abolished before the year 2006, as per the WTO agreement. Hence we have 3 years to gear ourselves for international competition. This is probably the last chance for rural entrepreneurs to organise themselves and convert this challenge in to an opportunity.

High Cost of Milk Production

What are our problems? Why are we threatened by the international dairy market? The main problems are high cost of milk production, high cost on milk processing, marketing and poor quality milk due to unhygienic milk handling. Hence we need to address these problems on priority. The cost of milk production in India is high because the average milk yield of Indian cows is only 978Kg as compared to 6273 Kg in Denmark, 5289 Kg in France, 5462 Kg in United Kingdom, 5938 Kg in Canada, 7038 Kg in USA and 11000 Kg in Israel. The weather condition in Israel are worse than India. The temperature in summer exceeds 47°C-48°C; while the temperature in winter is as low as 4°C-5°C. Inspire by such bad weather and severe water shortage, the average milk production of dairy cows is 11000 Kg/Lactation. Hence, there is good scope for more quantity of milk production per cow is possible in India.

High Cost on Milk Handling

Our dairy entrepreneurs get about Rs. 7-8 per at their village co-operative. This milk is handled at several levels by Co-operative or private till it reaches the main dairy located in a large city for pasteurization. The milk is then sent to consumers through various outlets. In this process, the consumers have to pay almost twice the farmgate price i.e. around Rs. 14-16. The present system is not only unhygienic but also expensive. There is good scope for reducing the number of agencies handling the milk to reduce the cost on handling.

Strategy for Conversion of Challenge into Opportunity

Reduction in Cost of Milk Production

It is necessary to immediate steps to reduce the cost of milk production by increasing the productivity of our animals. Animal Husbandry Department should assist the rural small entrepreneurs (Formers) in solving their problem time to time. Concurrent with improving genetic potential of dairy animals, necessary nutrient input has to be provided for maximizing the dairy production. Our Indian milk producers should try to get more quantity of milk per cow as like Israel milk producers. Production of more quantity of milk per cow will bring down the cost of production. More quantity of milk production per cow has been achieved through proper housing, feed and water management, apart from superior quality germplasm.

Reduction of Milk Handling Cost by Setting up of Direct Marketing Association with E-commerce facility

Rural small entrepreneur is also necessary to look for an alternative model of milk processing and selling. They should create Direct Marketing Association at the levels of village, union and district. The DMA will set up processing and retail outlet for local needs. It should sell fresh milk as well as value added items such as milk cream, condensed milk, dried milk, Malted milk, cultured milk, filled milk, butter, margarine cheese and ice-creams. These items can be sold in local markets and also exported to foreign countries through internet and E-Commerce. Why should a rural small entrepreneur come to town to sell his produce? E-commerce today provides the infrastructure to communicate and share information, between the buyers and sellers. Infotech is at the heart of marketing today. Information is extensively used to discover new markets and newer ways of marketing. E-commerce basically involves using a combination of intranet and internet to link sellers, suppliers, distributors, banks and customers where information exchange, price negotiation, order placements, delivery confirmation, billing and payments take place-online. It is essentially and evolving set of IT tools and implementation techniques, as well as the business strategies and practice necessary to do business electronically.

Internet solution companies assist to design website for you. They do services of Domine Registration, Web Design and Development and Hoisting. DMA should get website address by paying of appropriate fees to internic institution. The rural small entrepreneur can not get website address due to lack of funds, professionalism, internet etc. All rural small entrepreneur should become a member in the Direct Marketing Association. Those who are members in this Association can utilise the available facility of E-Commerce. It is enough to have an E-mail address for individual small rural entrepreneurs. They can link themselves to Direct Marketing Association Website through their E-mail address. Both the central and state Governments, Voluntary Organisation, Self Help Group and Enthusiastic computer learned entrepreneurs should come forward to setup Direct Marketing Association with E-Commerce facility. This will definitely reduce the cost on handling.

With reduction in the cost of milk production and cost on milk handling, the retail price can be reduced significantly and this can help the rural small entrepreneurs face the challenge of imported milk. The rural small entrepreneurs can send their dairy products to the any corner of the World, (International Market). Threat from the WTO will be converted into an opportunity by the rural small entrepreneur through the minimisation of cost of production and cost on handling of dairy products.

14

The Development of Entrepreneurism: The Role of Technical Consultancy Organisations

Dr. P.M. Meera Mohiadeen

Prelude

The most plausible way of viewing at the role of small enterprises in economic development is to see its relative position in terms of country's total production, employment and exports. It is proud to mentioned that the small-scale enterprises account for 40% of the gross value of the output in the manufacturing sector, about 80% of the total industrial employment and about 45% of the total exports of the country. It is noteworthy to mention that small scale enterprises have produced more than 7,500 different products.

The small-scale industries have registered phenomenal growth in terms of number, production, employment and exports over the years. Their number has phenomenally grown from 16,000 in 1950 to 32.25 lakhs in 1999-2000. While production has registered an increase of more than eighty times, employment grew by nearly five times over the period between 1973-1974 and 1999-2000. Growth in exports has been particularly commendable from mere Rs. 393 crores in 1973-74 to a mounting high figure of Rs. 53975 crores in 1999-2000. (See table. 14.1)

Table 14.1. Indicators of Growth in Small Scale Sector

Years	*No. of Units*	*Production (Rs. Crores)*	*Employment (Lakhs)*	*Exports (Rs. Crores)*
1973-74	N.A.	7,200	37.70	393
1977-78	2.96	14,300	54.00	845
1980-81	4.48	28,060	71.00	1,643
1985-86	8.55	61,288	96.00	2,769
1986-87	9.50	72,250	101.40	3,648
1987-88	10.48	87,300	107.00	4,373
1988-89	11.59	1,06,400	113.00	5,490
1989-90	16.59	1,32,320	119.60	7,626
1990-91	19.40	1,57,550	126.20	9,100
1991-92	20.00	1,60,000	126.00	12,658
1992-93	22.35	2,09,300	134.06	17,785
1993-94	23.84	2,41,648	139.40	24,000
1994-95	25.71	2,93,990	146.56	25,307
1995-96	27.24	3,56,213	152.61	36,470
1996-97	28.57	4,12,636	160.00	39,249
1997-98	30.14	4,85,171	167.20	43,946
1998-99	31.21	5,27,515	171.58	48,979
1999-2000	32.25	5,78,470	177.30	53,975

Source: Compiled from FASII Bulletin for Small Industry, Sep. 1996, vol. XXXV, No. 9. And Statistical Report of SMES in India, Dec. 1999, IBA Bulletin November, 2001 and Laghu Udyog Samachar, vol. XXIV to XXV, No. 9-2, April-Sep., 2000.

In spite of the above encouraging achievements there has also been gradual increase of the sickness and closures in this vital sector. The small and medium enterprises as a group experience the problems related to credit, infrastructure, raw material, technology, marketing, brand names etc. All these problems lead to make the units non-performing or sick ones. The table 14.2 shows that whereas there were only 21,882 sick units in 1990, the number has increased to 2,68,815 in 1995 (an increase of 12.28 times in 1995 over 1990). In absolute terms, the number of sick units

Table 14.2. Industrial Sickness in SSI Sector

Year	*Units*	*Amount Outstanding (Rs. In Crores)*
1980, December	23,149	306.00
1985, December	1,17,783	1,071.00
1988, December	2,40,573	2,141.00
1990, March	2,18,828	2,426.94
1991, March	2,21,472	2,792.04
1992, March	2,45,575	3,100.67
1993, March	2,38,176	3,443.00
1994, March	2,56,452	3,680.00
1995, March	2,69,000	3,547.00
1996, March	2,62,376	3,722.00
1997, March	2,35,032	3,609.00
1998, March	2,21,536	3,857.00
2000, March	3,06,000	4,313.00

Sources: Compiled from the Economic Times Data Bank p. 45. & Tata Services Ltd., Statistical Outline of India, 1997-98, Table. 91, p. 90. RBI Report on Currency and Finance, 1998-99, Vol. I, p. iv-8 RBI Currency and Finance, 1998-99, Table Ind. 7 & Ind. 8 p.p. iv-24 and iv-25.

as on March 1995 over 1990 was 2,46,933, which is a disturbing trend. Though the number of sick SSI units reduced in 1998 over 1995 still this number is very high. As on March 2000, more than 3 lakh SSI units are categorised as sick units covering a bank credit of Rs. 4313 crores. The above set back was the disincentive the new generation entrepreneurs and also it will affect the efforts of the existing entrepreneurs. Therefore, this malady is to be checked immediately because it might be affect the development of Entrepreneurism in the entire country.

Sickness in small scale industries is a cause for concern not only to the small scale business units; entrepreneurs but also to the development of powerful Entrepreneurism. Hence, the revival of the sick units should be taken on a priority basis by the Government. The immediate help to the sick units will be the provision of adequate credit through banks and financial institutions and takes necessary steps to restructuring or reconstruction of affected units. This will require financial commitment and policy changes. But the government has already been de-reserved the small scale sector and substantially reduce the plan outlay for the small scale industries and the protection comes to an end. At this juncture, a possible alternative is to counsel the sick units' entrepreneurs through the proper consultancy. Re-orient the small scale sick units are become imperative. For this purpose, the financial, organisational and technical reorientation is essential and this can be done through the proper amount of consultancy.

Need for Consultancy

Management Consultancy is becoming an indispensable service for revival of small scale industries. It is being considered as an essential aspect for upgrading knowledge, skills and attitudes of entrepreneurs. It helps them to achieve better performance and develop dynamic enterprises. Its contribution starts from pre-investment stage and continues though implementation and operation stage of enterprises. It is note worthy to mention S.S. Nadkarni's statement that "I do not know of any corporate problem where the solution decided upon, can not improve by a second look. If this involves a look from an outside agency, which has some experience and expertise in tackling problems it is all the more rewarding, to my mind a management consultant precisely fills this role.

Management consultancy is very wide field. It includes giving advice, conducting research, and testing attitudes and opinions, suggesting solutions to the problems and methods for organising work. The entrepreneurs require management consultancy at five stages namely 1. Pre-operative stage, 2. Take-off stage, 3. Post-operative stage, 4. Expansion stage and 5. Sickness stage.

Over the years, the number of management consultants and range of their services has been growing and the profession has built a strong base in India and abroad. The Small Industry Service Institute (SISIs) Technical Consultancy Organisations (TCOs) and Consultancy Service Cell (CSC) have been established by the Small Industries Development Organisation and All India Financial Institutions and Commercial Banks respectively, for providing consultancy services.

Besides, there are management departments in Universities, Professional management institutions, national and state productivity councils, and quality making centres and district centres. Later on private consultants, individuals as well as firms have also been joined the streams. SISIs and TCOs cover the whole gamut of activities related to a project cycle. On the other hand, CSCs concentrated their efforts on selected services of small enterprises to ensure productive use of the credit granted to them by commercial banks. To improve the designs of the products of small sale industries, the entrepreneur can approach the Industrial Design Cell and National Institute of Design. This Cell has been engaged in evolving new designs which are suitable for production in the small scale sector with its limited resources and mechanical and technical ability. The National Institute of Design organised training programmes for entrepreneur, graduates and designers. Apart from the above two there are hosts of private sector design companies like Elephant Design, Federal Technologies, Ohio Design, Incubis, Design Directions, etc. In contrast, the private consultants have no functional specialisation, location, boundaries and size wise restrictions. However, they help small-scale units only sparingly. They prefer larger and repetitive assignment for various reasons.

The Role of Consultancy

A network of Technical Consultancy Organisations (TCOs) was established by the all India financial institutions in the seventies and the eighties in collaboration with state level financial/development institutions and commercial banks to cater to the consultancy needs of small-scale industries and new entrepreneurs. At present there are 17 TCOs operating in various States, some of them covering more than one States? Table 14.3 shows the performance of the TCOs. It indicates that the TCOs mainly concentrated on the project profile and feasibility study. For example, out of 4104 consultancy assignments, 3451 (84.1%) assignments were for project profile and feasibility study during the period between 1993 and 1994. During the period between 1994 and 1995 it was 76.5%. These assignments were taken from the small-scale enterprises at the initial period i.e. pre-operation stage. Therefore, the entrepreneurs give more weightage to procurement of funds than management to increase the competence. It is concluded that the entrepreneurs were hesitated to consult the management consultant during the other phases of the business operation. Management consultancy is most needed by entrepreneurs who have started production but not yet stabilised. This is substantiated by the fact that sickness creeps into many small-scale units within two years of commencement a study of 472 cases which were finally disposed by the BIFR up to end of 1991 shows that the major cause of sickness has been mismanagement. Of the 472 cases, mismanagement was the causes of sickness in as many as 242 cases (i.e. 51%). Government policies were a cause in 145 cases (i.e. 35%) while labour problems were a cause of sickness in 52 cases (i.e. 11%) and time and cost over runs were a cause in 69 cases (i.e. 15%) (There is some overlapping of data as in some cases there was more than one cause of sickness). The small scale industrialists are rarely approaching the TCOs for diagnostic and turnkey assignments. TCOs are performing very well in all types of services but they will concentrate on other services. Further, the small scale industrialists generally trusted the views of consultant, if they are grey-haired. But, at present many professionals like C.A., I.C.W.A., and M.B.A., is young and

Table 14.3. Summary of Performance of TCOs

Type of Services	*1983-84*	*%*	*1984-85*	*%*	*1993-94*	*%*	*1994-95*	*%*
Feasibility study/Project reports/Profiles	991	63.8	1,019	57.9	3,451	84.1	2,171	76.5
Project Appraisals	338	21.8	356	20.3	205	5.0	178	6.3
Surveys/Studies (industrial potential surveys, market surveys, area development surveys etc.)	107	6.9	261	14.9	110	2.7	146	5.1
Modernisation/rehabilitation/diagnostic Studies	91	5.8	115	6.5	51	1.2	167	5.9
Functional industrial complex/turnkey Assignments	-	-	7	0.4	8	0.2	16	0.5
Other assignments/specific studies	26	1.7	-	-	279	6.8	161	5.7
Total	**1,553**	**100.0**	**1,758**	**100.0**	**4,104**	**100.0**	**2,839**	**100.0**

Source: IDBI Report on Development Banking in India, Industrial Development Bank of India, Bombay, 1994-95, p. 79.

energetic. The Consultancy charges are levied by the professional are not so high but the small-scale industrialist's attitude prevents to go to approach the professionals. Hence the small-scale entrepreneurs will have to change their attitude of knowing all things to there be many things they do not know. Therefore, it is imperative to consult the management consultant at the take-up stage to sickness stage. To reduce the incidence of industrial sickness in the SSI, the entrepreneurs should make detailed diagnostic study and point out the reasons for the sickness. The diagnostic report which must cover all the technical, management, economic, marketing, financial and other environment factors so that the bankers and financial institutions can identify the genuine reasons for sickness and try to help the small scale industrialist in right direction. For this purpose the entrepreneurs conduct the right type of consultant. But there is a general belief among the entrepreneurs that the availing of consultancy service during the sickness stage is not a must. Because they are not in a position to spare much amounts for consultancy services due to paucity of working capital. Therefore, in most cases the entrepreneurs not analysing the problems through the consultancy service and to submit rehabilitation draft to the financial institutions or a nationalised banks. Many entrepreneurs fail to realise the important contribution of a consultant in their unique situation namely sickness stage. Further, to prevent the industrial sickness, the small-scale enterprise owners should keep in touch with consultants and solve all the internal problems and make their units viable.

Another major reason for the sickness of the small scale units is the use of outdated technologies and designs. Till recently, most of the product manufactured in the small scale sector were either imitations of imported products, irrespective of any considerations of suitability of Indian conditions or were functionally bad. The small scale units often do not care about the changing tastes and fashions of the people. Accordingly redesigning the product, modernisation and rationalisation are urgently required in small scale industries. This task can be accomplished over by a network of technical assistance and advice through the National Institute of Design and Industrial Design Cell or host of private designers. But unfortunately the small scale industrialists not aware the significance of the designing and they are not concentrating in this aspect to reduce the industrial sickness. It is rightly pointed out that the National Institute of Design review committee observation here, "Although design is a real need in our society, it is not yet a sufficiently felt need. Those who most need design seem least aware of its significance". Hence, the government has taken necessary steps to educate the small scale industrialists to utilise the Industrial Designing Cell and National Institute of Design.

Conclusion

The incidences of industrial sickness in small scale enterprises are alarming. To reduce the sickness in small scale sector, it is imperative to consult the management consultants by the small scale operators and obtain the professional expertise in all the stages of the operation, especially under the sickness stage. Further, the TCOs and other management consultancy organisation are focussing their attention to remove the sickness in SSI sector through rendering of different types of consultancy services. Therefore, the small scale entrepreneurs are shedding their shyness to availing the consultancy services and going to avail all the consultancy services from the management consultancy organisations for running the SSI units as a viable one. If the sick units turn around into successful units there will be a chance to enter into the small scale business by the other entrepreneurs, the bank will provide more credit to the small scale enterprises. This will further be augmented the development of powerful entrepreneurism in the country.

References

S.S. Kahanka, *Entrepreneurial Development*, S. Chand and Company Limited, New Delhi, 1999, pp. 138-139.

Vivek Dholankar, *Management of Small Scale Industries*, Common Wealth Publishers, New Delhi, 1993, pp. 225-256.

M.S. Chhikara, *Small Scale Sector During Economic Liberation*, International Industries Annual, 1995, pp. 159-165.

S.K. Mishra & B.K. Puri, *Indian Economy*, Himalaya Publishing House, Mumbai, 2000, p. 627.

The Hindu Business Line 14th November, 2000, p. 7.

Business Today, *"Indian small business: languishing at death's door"*, 21st April, 2001, pp. 82-88.

J.C. Sandesara, *"Modern small industries, 1972 and 1987-88: Aspects of growth and structural change"*, Economic and Political Weekly, 6, February, 1993, p. 227.

M.S. Narayanan, *Industrial sickness review of BIFR's role*, Economic and Political Weekly, 12th February, 1994, Table. 2, p. 364.

Vasant Desai, *Dynamics of Entrepreneurial Development*, Himalaya Publishing House, New Delhi, 2000, pp. 505-518.

Vidya Viswanathan & Gina Singh, *Design makes an impression*, Business World, 22nd January, 2001, p. 21.

15

Future Entrepreneurism

S. Sivakumar

Abstract

This paper is for throwing much light on various opportunities that are available to enhance individual wealth as well as overall economy with new entrepreneurial opportunities. The emerging trends of entrepreneurism focuses the following knowledge areas:

- IT enabled services-call center
- Chemical services
- Modeling of living organisms as specimen to bio-medical R & D work
- Smart materials
- Radiation based food processing and miniaturization.

Introduction

The substantial gains in wealth are possible within the usage and diffusion of knowledge. Without skills, ideas may be irrelevant, and without ideas, there may not be necessity of new and better skills. The invention of writing, initially required the development of writing skills. Similarly, the widespread use of the computer is increasing the demand for computer literacy. New ideas spur the development of the skills required to use those new ideas. The beginnings of the age of entrepreneurship, the stirrings of a socio-economic convulse that has the potential to reconfigure everything that we have ever seen before. Sure, entrepreneurship has always existed. But it suddenly seems to have received a certain sense of exuberance. Fresh graduates, pin-striped executives who have dropped out of the corporate rat race, self employed professionals with big thinking make the Indian entrepreneurs growing by the day. But who will be tomorrow's entrepreneurs and what businesses will they be running? In the next decade we are likely to see the mushrooming growth of small, smart companies formed by young entrepreneurs with their roots in research and development. Their trump card will be knowledge, not financial muscle. It is often difficult to predict the future, but it is always worth the effort. We have selected a set of industries that will not only be important across the world, but also they are typically suited to the prospective Indian entrepreneurs. Companies in these areas may not necessarily develop state of the art technology, but are sophisticated enough to be called knowledge companies.

IT Enabled Services

Imagine this, you need an urgent product detail but be reluctant to spend hours trying to get through to the authentic person in the concerned company. Instead replace this with another scenario here all you have to do is placing a call to a specific number and have the problem dealt with. Makes the work much easier and more effective this is exactly what call centers do for you. This concept allows a person to call a single location instead of being shunted around. In the end the customer is happy and so is the firm it has retained the customer's goodwill. Today India is being touted as the hottest destination for IT enabled services especially call centers. In this context call centers are rapidly emerging as the corporates' main interface with the customers and have become a key business initiative, especially for segments such as airlines, mobile phone and paging services, e-commerce, hotels, banks and financial institutions. Fresh graduates with Computer knowledge and fluent in English have a new job option available to them. Everyday hundreds of aspirants line up to negotiate work opportunities with call centers as they are perceived to be good pay masters and thereby resulting in more employment opportunities.

The positive aspect in Tamil Nadu is that geographically most of the villages are within short distances of towns and cities. However, the limiting factor is the poor state of rural infrastructure for introduction of IT. We see hopes in technologies such as Wireless Local Loop in conjunction with optical-fibre backbones and other network devices along with community type of Internet centres with multiple roles. There is enormous scope for entrepreneurs to start ventures specifically addressed to rural IT.

Chemical Services

Chemical services are a lucrative business opportunity for Indian entrepreneur's atleast for the next 10 years. Services in chemistry such as custom synthesis, Contract research, Contract manufacturing or anything you like is a big, big business, ideally suited for Indian entrepreneurs. Like in the software industry the investments need not be big initially, but a few people, a shed, some instruments, and chemicals are just enough. In addition, you need to know some intricate chemistry and plant design. Indian Organic Chemicals Ltd. (IOCL) company is one such company near Mumbai having orders booked full for the next two years though it has been started only two years ago. Look a little more closely at the business. One of the most lucrative chemical services is synthesizing drug or chemical intermediates. An intermediate is a compound that can be converted into the final product very easily in few steps. Somebody needs to discover this process and some one else need to make it too, while the clinical trails are on.

The chemical services market estimated at between $5 billion and $10 billion now is expanding fast. And like in the software industry it's in the realm of the small company. Hundreds of profitable companies can sprout in the country provided they learn a few basic things apart from chemistry. Pharmaceutical companies are very fastidious. They insist on ensuring safety, environment friendliness and quality control.

Modeling Living Organisms

All scientists are fond of making models, which are stripped down versions of the actual thing. Models are useful in comprehending phenomena because they do away with experiments with living organisms. But when it comes to modeling, living organisms the situation is different. At IISc some scientists are trying to simulate living organisms. They may take a long time to achieve meaningful results, but an organism need not be seen in its entirety. In fact simulation can be more interesting and useful if restricted to parts not merely because it's easier and practical. In particular it has a contract from a US based company, Camitro Corporation, which develops computational models for what biologists call ADME (Absorption, Distribution, Metabolism and Elimination)/Toxicity studies. An ADME and toxicity study is silico is an ideal business opportunity for young skilled entrepreneurs in the country. Models help you to do studies in silico, using computers. Such studies reduce the time taken to bring a drug to the market. Using these models one can study how a drug behaves, without harming an animal or a human being. This business model is once again tailor-made for Indian entrepreneurs. You can setup shop with marginal investments, what you need is a Computational chemist, a Pharmacologist, a Physiologist and a Software Engineer. Some one need to do the business development as well, the market is big and could run into a few billions of dollars soon.

Smart Materials

If you want to look into the future one of the best venture to start with is an aerospace company, or better still an aerospace laboratory. Advanced technology often begins there and makes way into other spheres of life. National Aerospace Laboratories (NAL) in Bangalore designed and built an advanced two-seater plane, and being a research lab, it is trying to take it to the next generation. In the advance composites lab scientist G.N. Dayananda is developing a set of new flaps for the aircraft's wings. These flaps contain no hydraulics machinery. They are simply connected to a set of wires that contract when heated by an electric current, but come back to their original shape when cooled. When they contract the wires exert enough force to raise or lower the flaps. These wires made of titanium and nickel alloy called nitinol, help aircraft designers do away with hydraulics, thus reducing weight. Any weight reduction in an airplane is valuable's you can carry more passengers or do with less fuel. NAL will fit these flaps into the next generation two seater plane, *Hansa*.

However the property of an expanding and contracting material has hundreds of civilian applications. And herein lies a potential of starting large industry. Nitinol is a smart material more specifically it's a shape memory alloy, a material that can remember its shape and come back to it after the strain is removed. It can be useful in medical applications such as dental braces. The automobile industry has started using smart materials special fluids which change their flow characteristics under a magnetic field extensively for clutches and brakes. The global market for this is expected to be $200 billion a year in around six years. A good reason for entrepreneurs to start.

Radiation Processed Food Preservation

The research done at Trombay has demonstrated the advantages of food preservation by radiation processing. The process of food preservation by radiation offers several advantages over conventional food preservation techniques. The Government of India has approved radiation processing of certain food items both for export and domestic consumption. Two research and development irradiation facilities, one at Trombay and the other at Defence Laboratory in Jodhpur (Rajasthan), have been licensed for irradiating food items.

Spices Launched

In view of the advantages of radiation processing technology for spices, Annapurna Mahila Mandal, a women's cooperative, launched the sale of radiation processed spices under the trade name 'Purnanna' at their outlet SHRADDHA, at Dadar, on November 24, 2001. The radiation processed spices kept for sale at the counter by Annapurna Mahila Mandal, had good consumer response.

This endeavour will not only benefit public, but will also generate employment opportunities for more number of women. For radiation processing of spices and other products, the Spice Plant with an initial throughout of 20 tonnes/day, set up by BRIT at Navi Mumbai, has been operating since January 1, 2000. A commercial demonstration plant POTON, for the treatment of potatoes and onions and other products requiring low doses, is also under construction by BARC at Lasalgaon, Nashik District, Maharashtra. Private sector is being encouraged to set up similar plants.

As entrepreneurs could not provide for everything, provision of common facilities such as cold storage, testing laboratories etc. were thought necessary. During the current plan, a provision of Rs 650 crore has been made for the development of this sector. Thirty-six proposals for establishing industrial parks for food processing units have been sanctioned, according to the Union Minister for Food Processing Industries, Mr. N.T. Shanmugam. Among the 36 proposals sanctioned by the government 29 parks would be promoted by the government, six by the private sector and one as a joint venture.

Miniaturization is Key to Efficient Machines

This is straight from science fiction, Imagine machines so small that hundreds of them can be injected into your bloodstream. They are programmed to do specific tasks. 21st century will be a century of miniaturization. New fabrication techniques have made it possible to manufacture machines of only a few microns in diameter which will be one-thousandth a millimetre. When you make machines so small the price drops dramatically. The machines also consume little energy. And, we saw now they could be made to perform tasks so far undreamt of. Micromachines have become so important that they already have a name *Micro Electro Mechanical Systems* or MEMS.

Companies and market observers in the US are already talking about a market of $100 billion a year. You may be wondering of having such big opportunities for Indian entrepreneurs. MEMS are already being used as accelerometers (which detect acceleration) in an automobile. Traditional accelerometers consist of a sensor in conjunction with a lot of paraphernalia to analyse the information from the sensor. But if you have MEMS, a single machine will do everything imaging the reduction in space, weight and costs. As far as our country is concerned MEMS fabrication is not possible yet. India is still way behind other countries. The first MEMS fabrication is likely to be built by ITI in Bangalore, but India has no hope of catching up on MEMS manufacturing in the near future. However what we can do is designing of MEMS. Designing a MEMS will be a big opportunity for Indian companies. All you need is five people and a couple of workstations. There are small groups of researchers working on MEMS in various labs in the country. IISc, IITs, the Solid state Physics laboratory in Delhi and the Central Electronics Engineering Research Institute (CEERI) in Pilani. These researchers have created the initial MEMS knowledge base in the country.

16

"Poverty Stricken Rural Entrepreneurs" A Micro Study on Carpentering Sector

Mrs. A. Mary Grace
Dr. S. Maria John

India is one of the developing countries where the major portion of the population i.e. 74.28 per cent is living in 5,76,126 villages. The standard of living in villages continues to be poor. So there arises a necessity of developing the villages. In developed countries like Japan, Switzerland, Portuguese, Brazil, New Guinea, Uruguay, Paraguay, Liberia, Zimbabwe etc., the Gross National Product (GNP) growth rate is considered to be 6% and there exists economic stagnation. On the other hand there is an increase of GNP in the fast developing countries like Kazakhstan, Guinea, Tajikistan, Georgia, Mozambic, China, Vietnam, Madagascar and the like. (Survey conducted by the International Economics Magazine-Economist) In countries where the GNP rate is low there exists poverty. In India the GNP is only 6 percent.

Poverty is a social phenomenon in which a section of the society is unable to fulfill even to basic needs of life when a substantial portion of the society is being continuously below a certain level, that society is said to be plagued with mass poverty. The third world countries have pointed out the existence of poverty even in some packets of developed countries. Economists have differences in methodology in defining poverty and thus their estimates may vary in magnitude. But there is a general consensus in two things that,

(a) the percentage of population below poverty line has started declining as a consequence of the indirect benefit of high economic growth rate and also as a result of the impact of the direct programmes of poverty alleviation,

(b) the absolute number of poor has certainly increased over the years, since the major chunk of the poor reside in rural areas where there is low productivity and employment.

Determinants of Poverty

According to many studies, numerous variables have been identified as determinants of poverty. These factors have temporal and spatial variations in poverty. These factors include agricultural output, inflation rate, relative food prices, infrastructure facilities, non-agricultural employment and government's developmental expenditure.

An analysis in this regard has shown the results in percentage in Table 16.1.

The Indian economy, though considered to be a developing economy, has been facing many problems in connection with employment generation. Employment is generated by entrepreneurs of different nature. At present the various entrepreneurs doing the following works are affected to a marked extent, they are: Carpentry, Masonry, Pottery, Agricultural Farmers, Weavers, Road construction workers, Quarry workers, Blacksmith, Brick workers, Coir workers, Fishermen and the like.

Table 16.1. Determinants of Poverty

Sl. No.	Nature	Comment	%age
1.	Agricultural output	Agree	79
		Disagree	21
2.	Inflation rate	Agree	66
		Satisfactory	34
3.	Relative food prices	Agree	81
		Disagree	13
		Satisfactory	6
4.	Infrastructural faculties	Agree	89
		Disagree	11
5.	Non-agricultural employment	Satisfactory	43
		Disagree	57
6.	Governments Development expenditure	Agree	38
		Satisfactory	62

Source: Primary Data.

An attempt is made to have a micro study on the entrepreneurial possibilities created by carpentry entrepreneurs in Kanyakumari District. India has around 4 lakhs carpentry workers. Of these number, a majority of the workers are found in Tamilnadu alone.

The change of trend in carpentering has pulled down about 15 lakhs of carpenters to a pitiable condition in Tamilnadu. It was upto the recent past that a construction work was not carried over without the participation of carpenters. The major and vital role played by carpenters in the construction side has been set a part by the saw mills which appear to be the dragous in carpentering that they do the work within one hour for which the carpenters need 10 days.

The first hit fell on the carpenters when the Roof Cement Concrete system was introduced. Next, the Grill and Aluminum wires not only modernized the construction work but also keep carpenters 90 per cent away. The government also made carpenters' life worse by some laws that the public buildings should utilize either grill or aluminium wires. The same thing is followed in the construction undertaken by private schools, colleges, private companies and public industries.

Scientific developments in the construction side has absolutely swallowed the employment opportunities of carpenters. The recently introduced metal doors and thresholds have got a popularity among the public. Next, the molded ply wood designs have given the final hit on the carpenter community. They are available in the market at different levels of rates and have attracted all categories of people.

Tamilnadu has 28 districts. Of these, Kanyakumari District has more than 4 lakh families engaging in carpentry works. These workers depend on the entrepreneurs for their livelihood. They include the following.

1. Architectural workers - (doing only carving on wood)
2. Skilled workers - (doing all types of works except carving)
3. Semi-skilled workers - (doing partial work)
4. Helpers - (doing only preliminary works)

Sampling

An empirical study was carried on in Kanyakumari District. The District has four Taluks viz., Agasteeswaram, Vilavancode, Kalkulam and Thovalai. A study has revealed that, the entrepreneurs engaged in carpentry work are evenly spread in the district. Among the four Taluks, the total number of carpentry entrepreneurs out number in the Agasteeswaram Taluk. So the Taluk has been selected for study. Among the various blocks in the selected Taluk, five villages were selected where the ratio of this type of entrepreneurs is higher than other types. 25 workers from each category of carpentry workers were selected at random.

With the help of as interview schedule, factors affecting their personal identification like age, education, income, dependants, debts, hereditary nature and bonded life were analyzed as shown in Table 16.2.

Table 16.2. Personal Identification

Type	*Age*		*Education*		*Income (P.a.)*		*Dependants*		*Debts*		*Hereditary*	*bonded*
	Years	*No.*		*No.*	*Rupees*	*No.*		*No.*		*No.*	*No.*	*No.*
Architectural	20-25	11	Upto Std X	8	Upto 10,000	9	Below 5	9	Upto 10,000	4		1
	Above 25	14	Above Std X	17	10,000-30,000	8	Above 5	16	10,000-30,000	12	7	-
	-	-	-	-	Above 30,000	8	-	-	Above 30,000	9	-	-
Skilled	20-25	9	Upto Std VIII	11	Upto 10,000	11	3-5	6	Upto 10,000	0	-	-
	Above 25	16	Std VIII to X	14	10,000-20,000	8	5-8	9	10,000-30,000	15	8	2
	-	-	-	-	Above 20,000	6	Above 8	10	Above 30,000	7	-	-
Semi-Skilled	18-25	12	Upto Std VIII	16	Upto 7,500	12	3-5	8	Upto 5,000	5	-	-
	Above 25	13	Std VIII to IX	9	7,500-15,000	8	5-8	7	5,000-10,000	13	18	4
	-	-	-	-	Above 15,000	5	Above 8	10	Above 10,000	7	-	-
Helpers	Upto 15	9	Upto Std V	13	Upto 5,000	14	Above 2	25	Upto 5,000	9	-	-
	15-20	8	Std V to Std VIII	7	5,000-10,000	7	-	-	5,000-10,000	8	21	3
	20-25	4	Std VIII to Std XII	5	Above 10,000	4	-	-	Above 10,000	7	-	-
	Above 25	4		-	-	-	-	-		-	-	-
Total		100		100		100		100		-	-	-

Source: Primary Data No. = Number

It is inferred from table 16.2 that, majority of the workers except helpers, are above 25 years age group. The level of education exhibits that 45 (45%) of the workers have educational qualification above std VIII. The Income status reveals that 57 per cent of the workers' income is below Rs. 10,000 per annum. A majority of 53 per cent of the workers have dependants more than five. The indebtedness of the workers have revealed that 57 per cent of the workers have debts of above Rs. 10,000/- each. The table 16.2 also reveals that 21 helpers, 18 semi-skilled and 7 architectural workers live as bonded labourers.

The income of the workers is declining year after year. The number of dependants is also on the increase. So this situation results in regular borrowing to lead their life. Their debt position increases year after year. They could not make any investment in their business. Thereby a majority does it as a hereditary occupation knowingly or unknowingly 10 per cent of the carpentry workers are forced to live as bonded labourers.

Problems and Prospects

Knowledge updation

A majority of the carpenters in the study area is imparting the skill to their future generation. The mechanization introduced in the recent years have affected the community very severely. It is suggested that they can update their knowledge and can buy small machines to do the job. As they live below the poverty line the commercial banks should help them in this regard.

Diversification

It is a concept available in every field. The affected carpenters can generate skills in diversified economic activities like coir manufacturing, missionary, agricultural marketing, cultivation and various other sophisticated economic activities. The government agencies and voluntary agencies must engage skill formation.

Cooperatives

Starting of cooperatives especially for carpenters will definitely pave the way for their betterment. The cooperatives can impart latest technologies, give them job throughout the year by taking contract works, supply machines used in the work and diversified business and the like. So the members/carpenters will be able to avail all other common benefits rendered by other cooperatives.

Carpentry itself is a self employment business. Likewise one entrepreneur can also engage in other activities too. The Government is taking steps to develop all entrepreneurs in the form of granting subsidy and imparting latest technology related activities. The Government can take drastic steps to improve the downtrodden carpenters. The schemes introduced to help the poor rural have not covered the carpenters. Schemes exclusively for helping the carpenters and other affected workers could also be implemented. With the implementation of new beneficial schemes especially to the carpenters, the government can place these people in an elevated plane.

References

Dr. B.P. Tyagi—Agricultural Economics and Rural Development, Jai Prakashnath & Co., Meerut.

A.N. Agarwal, Indian Economy, 21st Edition, Wishwa Prakashan, New Delhi.

District Abstract 2002-2003, Collector's Office, Kanyakumari District.

Official Records of Department of Statistics, Government of Tamilnadu, Nagercoil.

17

Government Assistance and Entrepreneurial Development

B. Sella Raja

Introduction

There will be a lot of Entrepreneurial Development in a country where the government is committed to economic development and has clear-cut industrial policies. The supportive actions of the government such as creation of basic facilities, utilities and services and providing incentives and concessions are necessary for Entrepreneurial Growth. Such assistance on the part of the government also minimizes the risks of Entrepreneurs. On the other hand, there will be least Entrepreneurial development in a country if the government is not interested in economic development.

Need for Government Assistance

In India over the years, both central and state governments are extending various incentives and subsidies to motivate the people to start various businesses. These assistance make the environment more conducive to start many new ventures which result in decentralization of Economic power. Another objective of the Government with such assistance, is to correct regional imbalance and secure the industrialization of the backward areas of the country. Thus, the government by providing Non-Economic and Economic assistance, is trying to create the spirit of Entrepreneurship especially in the minds of the unemployed youth, which not only makes them employed but also contributes towards over-all economic development of the country. This paper intends to bring out the liberal concessions extended by the government which most of the common people and the unemployed youth are not aware.

Non-Financial Assistance

The non-financial Assistance generally includes identification of project-ideas, preparation of feasibility-studies and project-reports, identification of infrastructural gapes, providing for managerial, technical and marketing assistance etc... Such assistance is rendered by the government with the establishment of following institutions and Agencies:

1. Assistance in Identifying Business-Opportunities

The establishment of New units is always the toughest one. According to the study conducted by Institute of Economics, Hydrabad, 50% of business unit becomes sick because of the wrong selection of business. Here comes the role of District Industrial Centres (DIC) setup by the government to help the prospective Entrepreneurs to select a suitable venture. DICs have various project-reports readily prepared in advance to recommend right business on the basis of financial qualification, financial position etc. of the aspiring business people.

2. Assistance in the Form of Training Programmes

The government-owned financial Institution namely The Small Industries Development Corporation (SIDC) has been regularly conducting training programmes for new Entrepreneurs through DIC, TIIC, SFCs etc... The necessary trainings are given to the Engineers, the educated, the unemployed, Women, Artisans, Technicians, Physically

Handicapped, Weaker section of the community and the students.

3. Assistance in the Form of Infrastructural Facilities

The main problem of prospective entrepreneur in the initial stage is finding a site for his business. To assist the new entrepreneurs in this regard, the state governments establish a lot of industrial estates in different places. These estates provide needed facilities and suitable factory premises.

4. Technological Assistance

The Small Industrial Development Bank of India through its Technical Consultancy Organization (TCOs) assists the entrepreneurs to identify right technology for their business. At present, there are 17 TCOs all over the country.

5. Marketing Assistance

The success of entrepreneurs greatly depends on their ability and efficiency in marketing their products. All business units, in particular, smaller units, face a lot of marketing problems. Hence, the government is providing assistance to these small units to market their products in the following ways:

1. Director General of Supplies and Disposals purchases exclusively from the smaller business units to meet the various requirements of Central Government offices.
2. The Government is also extending marketing assistance to small units with reservation of certain items of goods for exclusive manufacture in small scale sector.
3. The Small Industrial Development Organisation (SIDO), is providing marketing assistance to smaller business units with the supply of marketing Intelligence and information by establishing Trading

Centres and by conducting exhibitions at different places to popularize the products manufactured by smaller units.

Financial Assistance

Finance is life-blood of any business. Infact, it's the availability of finance which enables the entrepreneurs to bring together other factors of production, namely land, labour, machinery and combine them to produce goods. The Government extends financial assistance in the form of incentives, subsidies soft loans etc., We are concerned with incentives and subsidies.

Incentive and Subsidy

One of the important objectives of Government policy is to correct the regional imbalances and secure the industrialization of backward areas of the country towards this end, the central and the state Governments have provided several incentives to enable the entrepreneurs to establish industrial undertaking in backward areas.

The term "Incentive" includes concessions, subsidies, and bounties. Subsidy refers to single lumpsum given by the Government to an industry. Subsidy is given to an Industry which is considered essential in the interest of the nation. Bounty denotes the financial aid, given by a Government to a specific industry to help it complete with other units in the home or overseas market. It is a bonus given in proportion to its output. The central and the state Governments have provided several incentives to enable entrepreneurs to establish industrial units in backward areas in the nation.

Information in brief about the incentives available for small scale industries in Tamil Nadu is given below:

A. ***Incentives by Government of Tamil Nadu Capital Subsidy***

1. 15% of the fixed capital investment subject to a ceiling of Rs. 15 Lakhs.

2. In respect of the units located in most backward taluks, capital subsidy will be 20% of the fixed capital investment subject to ceiling of Rs. 20 Lakhs.

B. *Special Subsidy*

1. 20% capital investment upto a ceiling of Rs. 35 lakhs for electronics, Rs. 20 lakhs for leather and Rs. 15 lakhs for other industries.
2. 8% export subsidy for leather and electronic industries.
3. In respect of the units using solar energy equipment and certain solar energy devices, 10% capital subsidy is eligible.
4. Old Tanneries which go in for Effluent Treatment plants will be eligible for 10% of the value of the assets to be created for the Effluent Treatment plants.

C. *Subsidy Schemes for Selected Categories of Industries*

The following types of industries setup anywhere in Tamil Nadu not covered either by the State or by the Central capital subsidy schemes are eligible to avail a subsidy of 10% of the value of the fixed assets or at the rate of Rs. 20,000/- per every regularly employed worker whichever is lower within an overall limit of Rs. 10 Lakhs.

1. Drugs and formulation of scheduled drugs
2. A select list of automobile ancillary units.
3. Manufacture of equipment, machinery, etc, to tap solar energy.
4. Export oriented gold jewellery making and diamond processing unit.
5. Special capital subsidy of 10% on the value of fixed assets subject to a ceiling of Rs. 5 Lakhs can be availed by the individual tanneries which have not availed any other Central/State subsidy.

D. Concessions Exclusively for SC/ST Entrepreneurs

1. Promoter's contributions reduced to 15%.

2. Interest on term-loans is reduced by 1.5%

3. State Industries Promotion Corporation of Tamil Nadu (SIPCOT) will directly participate in the share issues and take maximum possible shares.

4. SIPCOT prepares the feasibility reports at subsidized rates to the prospective entrepreneurs.

E. New Anna-Marumalarchi Thittam

The Tamil Nadu Government in the year 2002 issued an order for the implementation of the New Anna-Marumalarchi Thittam (NAMT). The order spells out incentives under a special package scheme, which is exclusive by for agro-based industries including processing of horticultural produce, flower-based extracts, coir and food-processing.

It provides 15% subsidy on investment in plant and machinery, limited to Rs. 15 Lakhs per block in all the 385 blocks. A low tension power tariff subsidy of 30%, 20% and 10% respectively for the first 3 years, a generator subsidy of 15% and 5% capital subsidy for employing more than 50% women in the work force.

The Incentives by Central Government

The Central Government has declared 247 districts as backward areas eligible for the subsidies. The programmes of assistance drawn up for setting up industries in the selected backward areas are presented below:

A. Concessional Finance

All India Financial Institutions namely IDBI, IFCI and ICICI extend financial assistance on concessional terms to all industries located in the 247 districts selected by the government. The concessions are in the form of lower-interest rate, lower-underwriting commission, initial-

moratorium period up to 5 years, longer-amortizations of 15 to 20 years and participation in the risk capital on selective basis.

B. *Central Investment Subsidy*

The granting of cash subsidy on the capital investment is called capital investment subsidy. It will be usually in the form of outright grant of 10% to 20% of the amount of capital invested in the industrial units in the specified backward areas subject to a ceiling.

C. *Seed-Capital Assistance*

The objective of the scheme is to create new generation entrepreneurs who have the requisite traits of entrepreneurship but whose financial resources are limited. It is operated through the agency of notified SIDCs and SFCs. IDBI also assists directly to the entrepreneurs under the scheme. The actual amount of seed capital assistance is determined on the basis of gap in the equity required for the project or short fall if any in the prescribed minimum promoter's contribution after taking into account his own contribution, and from other sources, and subsidies and incentives. The amount of seed-capital assistance for project shall not exceed Rs. 15 Lakhs.

18

Information Technology in Global Entrepreneurship

Dr. E. Mubarak Ali
Dr. A.M. Mohamed Sindhasha
Prof. A.R. Mohamed Ismail
M. Abdul Hakkeem

Introduction

With the emerging trends, Information Technology holds the key for success in the twenty-first century. With the winds of change sweeping across the globe, only computerization and professionally trained manpower will ensure success with higher standards of innovation and customer service. The increased acceptance of Internet has created the need to handle enormous amount of information for economic growth of individuals and nations.

With an ever growing demand for Information Technology professionals, the opportunities are aplenty for the aspiring youth. (With universal acceptance of the fact that "Indians are gifted with superior intellect and analytical mind". India is expected to play a very vital role in growth of the Information Technology industry worldwide. To achieve this, one must create a great pool of computer literate manpower. Also with on going liberalization and all round computerision in Government and private sector.) India is on threshold of a great Information Technology explosion.

All these factors have only increased the need for trained manpower and to sustain growth in this rapidly changing high-tech world, one must generate the world class manpower in not only Information Technology but also in other important areas of business management technology, science and other service industries.

Information Resource

Information is being worshipped today by ritually every one—be it organisations, government, individuals or professionals. The worship is supposed to provide a sense of security, mental peace, professional success, prosperity and even health.

Information is a versatile commodity. It enhances decisiveness analytical skills and bridges the unknown. It is the fountain that nurtures the personal growth, innovation and development. It provides the only grip in times of mega-acceleration. Information is personal power, it helps a person command respect.

The role of information in the economy is well established. It works like lubricating oil to make the system work better. It ensures wise decisions and can provide most sustainable competitive advantage.

Globalisation

The Globalisation ensued by liberalization policy of the Government of India has been instrumental in bringing out metamorphical changes on the economic front. Economic impact as a by product has social impact too. We now speak in terms of trade across the countries. The distance between the countries has been cut short and they are called as global villages. The keen competition posed by global players have forced firms to perform extremely well by keeping quality, cost and delivery as the watch words. The objective is keep the customer not only satisfied but delighted.

Globalisation does not mean having globes on the desktops of the Government and private offices. It refers to a movement. It refers to a free, uninterrupted international trade, characterised by global competition, freedom of mobility of capital, technology, knowledge, material and men including entrepreneurs.

Entrepreneurship can be defined as an ability to discover, create or invert opportunities and exploit them to the benefit of the society, which in turn, brings prosperity to the innovator and his organisation.

From the social and macro-economic perspective, it is held that the economic development of any nation is a direct function of the number of high quality innovators and entrepreneurs it supplies. This, inturn is dependent upon the desire for new and better products that the society demands and accepts.

A virtuous circle is thereby created resulting in all-round economic development and improved standard of life. Following liberalization and global competition, wealth creation is assuming paramount importance. As a result, the concept of entrepreneurship is receiving closed attention.

Global Competition and Entrepreneurial Opportunities

As Indian business globalises and interlinks itself with the world, the nature and range of business opportunities as well as challenges for India entrepreneurs are increasing. Competition is no longer between local firms, the present day competition is predominantly in the classical schumpeterian-type. It means that organisational and technological innovations, superior product quality and customer satisfaction are major determinants of firm- level competitiveness in the global market place. In a globally competitive environment, customers have a choice, and, therefore, look beyond buying commodities. They increasingly desire better value in tangible as well as intangible forms.

One does not become an entrepreneur by the mere act of starting or owing an enterprise. More important is the nature, degree and extent of innovations that the entrepreneur introduces and that to on a continuous basis.

In view of the changing environment, the need for a global entrepreneur with innovative outlook is now greater than ever before. Global entrepreneurs with innovative outlook always search for changes, respond to it and exploit as an opportunity. They are the ones who can make a difference, while ordinary managers are effective only in managing stable, routine and cost-efficient business. Global entrepreneurs are high achievers. They possess an idea or a distinct way of doing things. They show greater openness to experience and they have a more internal focus of evaluation.

Thus, a global entrepreneur must be a dynamic professional. He must have the ability to combine risk-taking with risk-managing, infuse academic regour to practical vigour, merge cold analysis with creative synthesis learn from hindsight to build a distant foresight and exhibit spontaneous verve with steely nerve.

Internet

The Internet is a real entity. An Internet is an open-ended network of computer and communication networks that now encircle the globe, with the greatest concentration of network, computers and users located in different parts of the country. There is no single administrative authority that owns, controls or manages the Internet, yet its users clearly benefit from access to information resources and services from around the world that can be brought to their desktop computers and their fingertips.

To use the Internet one should understand two basic concepts, such as, everything is connected together and every computer or other device connected to the Internet has a unique address. These two facts make it possible for one to use his computer to exchange data with any other computer on the Internet. Everything that happens on the Internet is some form of data transfer from one computer to another. The opportunities presented by the channel seem to be reality apparent by allowing for direct links to anyone anywhere.

Internet and Entrepreneurial Opportunities

We are living in the age of information revolution. The revolution brought about by the information or knowledge in the global scenario is by most part because of Information Technology. With the advent of Internet in the field of Information Technology, even the remotest village has now the possibility of tapping a global store of knowledge the dream of anyone living a century ago. Above all, the information flows quickly and cheaply.

The establishment of global entrepreneurial system presupposes the search for and selection of business ideas from all possible sources. Internet, as a source of information of business, has many uses like getting technical support for product, communicating and collaborating on projects. One can market and sell products, provide technical support and exchange product information. With its millions of inter connections, Internet can help a business seek advice from industry experts around the world. Besides this, one can access his business from anywhere in the world.

Internet provides excellent opportunity for the existing and prospective entrepreneurs to exchange information across the world.

One Mr. B. Shrinivas, an entrepreneur from Tamil nadu (He is in Chennai, his web address is www.pppindia.com) offers a ppp scheme. This means plans, proposals and projects.

People around the world, can get information about a wide range of products and services comprising of silk sarees, handicrafts, preparation of South Indian food items. The products are actually displayed in the screen with their distinctive features say colour, size, quality, price etc.

Any one who is interested in these products and services can place order through Internet. Mr. B. Srinivas, has been successfully marketing these products and services.

To cite another example, McMillan publishing Co., provides "Online library facility". An individual gets the accessibility for 5 books in his personal shelf in Internet for a period of one month. He can read and if necessary download any number of pages. This is an innovative approach adopted by this company in marketing its publications.

These two examples explain how good an entrepreneur can make global marketing opportunities.

Making of the Global Entrepreneur—Implications and Challenges

The making of the global entrepreneur has its implications at four levels namely, firm, industry, policy and management and technological education.

I. At the Firm Level

There is a felt need for improving the entrepreneurial behaviour inside the firms, at the corporate level. It has not taken roots yet in a substantial degree. The top management has to provide such an environment and structure. The global entrepreneur must get the desired challenges. He must be able to stretch himself and upgrade his skills by in-house training. It must allow individuals to invest in themselves by suitable cross-functional interactions.

II. At the Industry Level

Several Chambers of Commerce, Trade Associations

and representative industry groups will have to adopt a strategic approach in order to ensure that Indian firms benchmark beyond what exists. They should be able to set the standards for the rest of the world.

III. At the Policy Level

The general environment now is gradually becoming supportive to well-qualified and competent entrepreneurs. Especially in this context, educational and research institutions act as nurseries for providing world-class engineers, scientists and managers. These must be preserved and run autonomously, entrepreneurially and professionally. Apart from that managerial, technical and scientific manpower, the global entrepreneurs as key builders of nation's competitiveness should be recognised and their contribution should be acknowledged and given due respect.

IV. Management and Technological Institutions

The role of national management and technology institutes also has its significance in this context. Their commitment to professionalism, excellence and innovation assumes a critical dimension. These institutions will have the responsibility to supply the requisite number of dynamic global entrepreneurs who enjoy societal legitimacy. It is for such institutes to design courses and develop fresh teaching material for the making of a globally competitive entrepreneur.

Apart from this, research work needs to be carried out to assess the impact of organizational variables such as structure, strategy and culture, on the performance of business enterprise, in connection with making of global entrepreneurs.

Conclusion

Opportunities for global entrepreneurs have been increasing day by day under the changing environment. Whether an entrepreneur is currently a global entrepreneur or dream of becoming one, embracing the Authentic Entrepreneur traits has many advantages. He should remove the traditional entrepreneurial stigmas and allow himself more room for growth. So if the entrepreneur is ready to step forward and declare that he desires to live a meaningful and wealthy life, then it is time to make himself move. The entrepreneur has to shift the perspective and become an Authentic Global Entrepreneur. The making of such authentic global entrepreneur would reward the individuals themselves, the firms the industry, the economy and the society as a whole.

19

Floriculture—Problems and Prospects

Dr. S. Maria John
Dr. K. Andivelu

India is a land of villages in which resides about 80% of its population. It is endowed with natural wealth of plant materials, which are of great floricultural importance and significance. Large collections of beautiful plant species like those of orchids, rhododendrons, primula, camellia etc., are found wild in the Himalayan and other mountainous regions. Kashmir valleys and the famous valley of flowers are also rich source of indigenous flowers.

Flowers and gardens for long have been important in India for aesthetic, economic and social values. Economic flowers are those flower crops, which are grown on a commercial scale as field crops in certain selected areas of the state for supply of flowers to markets. In Tamil Nadu, Jasmine, Crossandra, Chrysanthemum and Rose are grown on a large scale and a few other crops like artismiske, origanerum, tuberose and marigold are also grown though to a smaller extent.

The commercial importance of the floricultural products mainly consists of cut-flowers and ornamental foliage plants. The world trade is estimated to be around $ 13 billion in 1981. Developed countries account for more than 90% of the total trade in floricultural products.

The floricultural products have the property of cooling the body and are often use in eye lotions and eye drops for their soothing qualities Various flowers are used to produce varieties of products. Among the various flowers used jasmine and rose play a major role. Hence floriculture relating to rose and jasmine are chosen for the study. Rose oil and Gulkand are derives from rose petals. Gul- Roghan is rose hair oil derived from rose petals. Roses are also used to prepare pot-pourri, rose vinegar, wine, jams, jellies and syrups.

The natural oil of jasmine is used in high-grade perfumes and almost all superior perfumes contain at least a small quantity of jasmine oil. It is used for perfuming luxurious soaps and cosmetics, mouthwashes and dentifrices, bath salts and tobacco.

The raw materials used for the production of the above said products, namely the flowers are highly perishable and hence require careful handling and disposal and therefore require a local market. The road and rail transports are also not economical and convenient. The cultivation of such plants remains localized for many varieties of flowers are produced depending on different soil and climatic conditions.

The demand and supply are also fluctuating and not steady. The climatic conditions very often deceive the cultivators for the frequent failure of monsoon. The product viz. the flowers, are sold to the customers through a very wide channel of distribution. So the middlemen in the market also play a dominent role in selling the product. The market structure is also not suffered a lot from many aspects. They have to be facilitated in all aspects. Hence a study of this nature is very essential.

Objectives

The objectives of the study are:

(*a*) To identify the risks involved in the production and marketing of flowers by studying the structure of flower market.

(*b*) To analyse the role played by the various channels of distribution involved in marketing of flowers.

Sampling

According to all India national sample survey conducted by ICAR in the recent years flowers are grown in about 4000 hectares for commercial purposes with an annual production of 10500 tonnes of cut flowers worth Rs. 9.26 crores, sold annually in the markets of Mumbai, Kolkata, Chennai, Bangalore and Delhi. In Tamil Nadu Madurai is the largest producer providing livelihood to 10000 persons.

Kanyakumari District stands 4th in flower production in the state. The annual rank varies according to some conditions. Of the four taluks in the District, Thovalai taluk occupies the major share of flower production. This taluk is endowed with good soil, which is suitable for flower cultivation. As the cultivable lands are located between mountains, the temperature and the climatic conditions are favourable for their growth and marvelous production.

More than 100 cultivators are growing various types of flowers. The total flower cultivators in the District employed more than 1000 workers. The taluks for the purpose of the study is divided into 4 blocks and by applying stratified random sampling technique 20 cultivators were selected.

It is an empirical study based on survey method. Primary data were collected from the selected sample members with the help an interview schedule for the purpose of analysis.

Role Played by Channels of Distribution

A channel of distribution for a product is the route taken by the title to goods as they move from the producer to the ultimate consumer. It brings profit to all the parties concerned. It is very essential as the customers are scattered. The channels of distribution shrink the gap between the customer and the producer. In flower channel of distribution, there are many parties who earn a lot in total, than the producers. The table 19.1 explains about the various parties involved.

Table 19.1. The market players in the channel of distribution for flowers and their share of profit

(Figures in percentage)

Sl. No.	*Market Players*	*Block 1*	*Block 2*	*Block 3*	*Block 4*	*Average*
1.	Cultivators/Producers	48	59	60	47	53.50
2.	Wholesale agents	15	12	14	10	12.75
3.	Commission agents	15	13	11	14	13.25
4.	Village traders	12	10	06	13	10.25
5.	Shop salesmen	10	06	09	16	10.25
6.	Customers	—	—	—	—	—
		100	100	100	100	100.00

Source: Primary Data.

Wholesale agents: Usually moneylenders

Commission agents: Sub agents of wholesale agents. They supply flowers to village traders and salesman who sell sitting through shops (either owned or leased or hired daily infront of main big shops)

It is revealed from the about table 19.1 that an average share of profit of 53.50 is enjoyed only by the cultivators. But it is to be noted that only out of this share, they have to meet their family maintenance, interest on borrowed capital, cultivation expenses and other miscellaneous expenses. The wholesale agents are very often acting as moneylenders to these poor agriculturists. Comparatively, the commission agents get a higher share than all other middlemen on an average. They get a share of profit without any long-term investment. But though, there is long term investment by the cultivators, their share of profit is less.

Structure of the Flower Market

Marketing is the ultimate business transaction, which is aimed at a profit. As flowers are perishable in nature, they require quick disposal. The flower market consists of a group of dealers. They are the growers (sellers) and buyers. As the producers cannot concentrate on direct sales to the ultimate customers, many dealers crop in. The method of sale of flowers from the following categories of salesmen.

Table 19.2. Method of sale of Flowers

SL. No.	*Pattern of sales*	*% of Sales to Different Patterns*	*% of sales on the first day*	*% of sales on the next day*	*% of unsold/ waste**	*Total percentage*
1.	Flower stalls in Towns	34	78	16	6	100
2.	Flower stalls in Villages	10	82	14	4	100
3.	Platform vendors	13	66	33	1	100
4.	Head load Hawkers	8	100	—	—	100
5.	Hawker sat bus shops	9	98	—	2	100
6.	Hawkers using bicycle	8	95	5	—	100
7.	Direct to business men (Industries)	12	—	—	—	—
8.	Cut Flowers	6	98	—	2	100

Source: Primary data. *Waste pertains to jasmine only.

The above table 19.2 tells us about the average ratio of distribution to various categories of salesman and also the average percentage of the flower sold on the first day of purchase, selling the unsold on the next day and the total unsold i.e. the waste.

It is evident from the table 19.2 that the established flower stalls in the towns and villages are also to sell unsold flowers on the next day. They suffered a little loss from the unsold waste. This is because they do not wander here and there to sell them at various places. They have only limited area of sales. They depend on the floating population only.

Vendors sitting on platform sell nearly 33% of the supply the next day, because they also depend only on the floating population. They too suffer little loss from waste for they try to sell the flowers, at least in second day at a less cost.

The Hawkers who carry the flowers by head and sell face less risk as, they do not buy more than the demand. These sellers have regular customers. Some hawkers make use of selected bus stops to sell flowers. They buy from the commission agents and sell to travellers who travel by four and two wheelers. They also do not buy more than the current demand. About 72% of this type of hawkers are daily employees of the commission agents. In the district, only 6% of the total production of rose and Jasmine are sold to floricultural industries.

Problems/Risks Faced by the Cultivators

The flower cultivators in the sample district face the following problems. The percentage to total of each risk is also given in Table 19.3.

Suggestions for Overall Development of Flower Cultivators

The Table 19.3 clearly indicates the sufferings of the flower cultivators on many grounds. These sufferings can be mitigated only by resorting to the establishment of:

1. Flower Co-operative societies and
2. Self-Help Groups among the flower cultivators.

These organizations may solve, in the following manner, their production and marketing problems.

(a) The establishment of the above organizations may ensure timely credit facilities to the cultivators either from the government or from nationalized banks. Such loan facilities may be made available at the lower rate of interest and without and collateral security. These measures may help the cultivators to come out of the clutches of the local moneylenders.

Table 19.3. Nature of Risks in Production and Marketing of Flowers

Sl. No.	*Particulars*	*Percentage*
1.	Failure of Monsoon	77
2.	Lack of adequate manure at subsidized cost	98
3.	Absence of an organized Flower co-operative society	100
4.	Non-availability of regulated market	69
5.	Presence of an unorganized channel of distribution	93
6.	Fragmentation and subdivision of land	62
7.	High cost of Agriculture	74
8.	High cost of Pesticides	89
9.	Owned/Leased land	82
10.	Lack of knowledge regarding modern techniques of production	68
11.	High cost of labour	75
12.	Financial Problems	70
13.	Low earnings	69
14.	Large size family	57
15.	Low savings	71
16.	Poor hygienic conditions of surroundings	63
17.	Excess medical expenses	51
18.	Drinking (Alcohol) habit	68
19.	Poor modes of transportation	77
20.	Lack of crop insurance	84

(b) The inputs like seeds, fertilizers, pesticides etc. may be procured in bulk by availing both subsidy and discount facilities. This measure will reduce the cost of cultivation of individual cultivators.

(c) As the flowers cultivated by the growers may be sold after assembling the output at a single point, such bulk assembling may facilitate

trading which may yield more prices to the cultivators. Likewise the transportation of flowers in bulk to the marketing center with the help of the vehicles supplied through flower co-operative societies will considerably reduce the transportation cost.

(d) When the cultivators organize co-operative societies or self-help groups among themselves, they can go for value addition to their products. They can do it by establishing separate unit for extracting oil from the flowers, which attract higher prices in the overseas market. This is more profitable especially when the supply of flowers exceeds the required local demand, which may take place during the peak flower supply seasons.

(e) Flower cultivators can generate additional income with the maintenance of adequate number of bee-hives for collecting honey in the flower cultivated areas, which does not cost more. At present honey marketing brings foreign exchange. This trade takes place in the district in a large-scale manner. As the honey has steady market, the cultivators are assured additional income in addition to the earnings out of main business of flower sales.

(f) The floriculture is undertaken with forming of self-help Groups to contribute some fixed amount every month towards a common fund and this fund becomes sizeable one, the nationalized banks may be coming forward to grant further loans on the basis of above accumulated fund. Thus the development of floriculture will not become stagnated. Even co-operative societies are formed; the same procedure may be adopted for further development of flower cultivators.

When all the above said suggestions are effectively implemented, the poor flower cultivators will surely get a better hand in the society. At present as the flower export yields only a little foreign exchange, there is every possible chance of enhancement.

REFERENCES

Handbook of Agriculture, Indian Council of Agricultural Research, New Delhi, 1980.

Bose T.K. and Arora J.S. Commercial Flowers, Calcutta, Bombay and New Delhi, Oxford and IBH Publishing Company 1987.

Seasons and Crops Reports, the Directors of Statistics/Government of Tamil Nadu, Chennai 1985, 86 and 87.

India 1990, A Reference Annual Publications Division, Ministry of Information and Broadcasting, Government of India.

20

Institutional Support to Rural Entrepreneurs

S. Jegadeesan

Introduction

India's economy based on the Rural Economy conditions. In order to develop the economy it has to develop the rural area. In every respects by creating more entrepreneurs in rural area, there is a possibility of increasing employment opportunities. As a result the per capita income of the country will also increase. The small-scale industries established by entrepreneur have been playing a major role in India's industrial and economic development. This sector has over the years developed as an important constituent of the Indian Economy in terms of its share in employment output and exports. Thus it made significant contribution to the development of rural and backward areas. The Government has provided the various types of assistance for the promotion of entrepreneur in rural areas.

Types of Government Assistances

1. Financial Assistance.
2. Marketing Assistance.
3. Exports Assistance and
4. Consultant Assistance.

Financial Assistance

To provide Financial Assistance to entrepreneurs, the Government has setup a number of special institutions. They are classified as

1. National Level Financial Institutions.
2. State Level Financial Institutions.

National Level Financial Institutions are as follows:

1. Industrial Financial Corporation of India (IFCI).
2. Industrial Credit and Investment Corporation of India (ICICI).
3. Industrial Development Bank of India (IDBI).
4. Industrial Reconstruction Bank of India (IRBI)
5. Small Industries Development Bank of India (SIDBI)
6. Export- Import Bank of India (EXIM).
7. Unit Trust of India (UTI).
8. Life Insurance Corporation of India (LIC)

State Level Financial Institution

1. State Financial Corporations (SFC)
2. State Industrial Development Corporation (SIDCS)
3. Tamil Nadu Industrial Investment Corporation Limited (TIIC)

The above financial Institution play an important role in the economic development of our country. The bank is primarily a financial agency for providing medium and long term capital, not only to the private sector but also to the public sector. It discovers investment projects, under-takes the preparing of project reports, provides technical advises and management services. It is a multi-purpose institution.

Marketing Assistance

Many incentives are provided both by the central and state Government to promote the growth of small scale industries and also to protect them from the onslaught of the large-scale sectors and foreign competitor. Among the various marketing assistance given to small-scale industries the following deserve special mention.

1. Reservation
2. Preference in Government purchase
3. Price preference
4. Supply of raw material
5. Excise duty.

Reservation

To protect the small-scale Industries from the competition posed by large-scale industries. The Government has reserved the production of certain items exclusively for the small-scale sectors. The number of items reserved for the small-scale sector stood as 836.

Preference in Government Purchases

The Government as well as Government organizations shows the preference in procuring their requirements. From the small-scale sector. For instance, the Director General of Supplies and Disposals purchases 400 items exclusively from the small-scale sector.

Price Preference

The SSI units are given price preference upto a maximum of 15 per cent in respect of certain items purchased both from small-scale and large-scale units.

Supply of Raw Materials

In order to ensure regular supply of raw materials, imported components and equipments. The government gives priority allocation to the small-scale sector.

Excise Duty

The SSI units are provided with the excise duty concessions to registered and unregistered units. They graded scale of production depending upon their production value. Hundred per cent exemption is granted upto a production value of Rs. 30 Lakhs in a year and 75% of normal duty is levied on production value. Exceeding Rs. 30 Lakhs but not exceeding Rs. 75 Lakhs of the production value exceeds Rs. 75 Lakhs, normal rate of duty will be levied.

Export Assistance

Many facilities are provided both by central and state Government to SSI units. Towards; Exports above facilities provided to manufacture Exporter, or Exporters. The following are also available to Indian Exporters:

1. Income tax Exemption
2. Concessional Rate of Interest for Finance to Exporters
3. Duty Draw back
4. Excise Rebate
5. Supply of Raw Materials.
6. 100% Export Oriented Units. (EOUs)
7. Freight Subsidy.

Income Tax Exemption

Under Sec. 80 HHC of Income tax Act 1961, 100% Income Tax Exemption is given to exporters. This section has been amended so as to phase out deduction over a period of five years from the assessment year 2000-2001. Now 50% deduction of Income tax is allowed for the assessment year 2003-04 and 30% deduction from the income of the units for the assessment year 2004-05; no deduction shall be allowed in respect of the assessment year 2005-06 onwards.

Concessional Rate of Interest of Finance to exporters

As per the RBI guidelines the exporters are eligible for pre-shipment at an interest rate not exceeding 10% upto a period of 180 days. The rate of interest is 12% from 181 days to 360 days. The exporters are also eligible for post shipment finance and 12% interest from 91 days to 180 days.

Duty Draw Back

The manufacturer has to pay

1. Import duties on raw materials and components imported.
2. Excise duty on the items manufactured in India.

If his products are exported from India he is entitled to get refund of the above two duties as per the customs and Central Excise Duty Draw Back Rules, 1971. Duty draw back is allowed only if the imported raw materials are used for the production of exported goods.

Excise Rebate

Finished goods which are subjected to excise duty for some consumption. They are exempt from duty when they are exported. The scheme is also applicable where exported goods contain excisable goods in their manufacture. The exporter can avail of this facility under bond or he can claim refund after the duty is paid.

Supply of Raw Materials

Units engaged in exports are given priority in the allotment of scarce raw materials such as steel. In certain cases, the raw materials are arranged to be supplied at International prices much below the internal prices.

100% Exports Oriented Units

Units undertaking to exports their entire production of goods may be setup under the Exports Oriented Units (EOU) scheme or Export Processing Zone (EPZ) scheme.

Some of the benefits available for EOU/EPZ units are:

- Developed plots/ready-buildings to suit the project requirements.
- Single point clearance of new projects within 40-65 days.
- No licence fee is required for import of capital goods, raw materials, consumables, spares etc.
- Duty free import of capital goods.
- Complete exemption from income tax on profits for a period of five years.
- Concessional finance is available for investment and working capital.

Freight Subsidy

Air freight subsidy is also allowed on exports of leather goods. Ocean freight subsidy is also available to exporters of bananas.

Consultancy Assistance

State Government and Central Government provided consultancy assistance to entrepreneur/SSI units.

There are:

1. Technical service.
2. Training facilities
3. District Industries Centers (DICs)

Technical Service

The small industries development organization provides technical consultancy services to SSI units. In order to provide the necessary technical input to rural industries. Technical consultancy organization renders consultancy services to SSI units at a subsidized rate. The small entrepreneurs proposing to set up rural cottage, tiny at a low cost from the technical consultancy organizations. They have to pay only 20% of the fees charged by a technical consultancy organization.

Training Facilities

It provides more training facilities to entrepreneur by following organization:

- The Entrpreneurship Development Institute of India
- Financial Institutions
- Commercial Bank
- Technical Consultancy Organization and
- National Small Industries Corporation Ltd. (NSIC)

District Industries Centre (DICS)

DIC is set up in each district the DIC provides and arranges a package of assistance and facilities for credit guidance, supply of raw materials, marketing, conducting seminar, exhibition etc.

Self Employment Opportunities

The person who has following attitudes may be said to have entrepreneurship quality which are

1. Self confidence
2. New innovation
3. Hard work
4. Dignity
5. Adventure

There are various self employment opportunities:

1. Mushroom cultivation
2. Herbal cultivate
3. Fish farm
4. Poultry farm

5. Dairy Farm
6. Sericulture Cultivations
7. Make Mineral Water
8. Marketing Agency
9. Two wheeler and Four Wheeler Trainings
10. Two wheeler and Four Wheeler Service centre
11. Promote yoga center
12. Labour Contract
13. Fancy Store
14. Fancy State
15. Hire service of agricultural equipments.

Conclusion

I conclude Gentleman both Central and State Governments are providing number of services to the budding and prospective entrepreneur to undertake new venture as well as expansion activities. However, these are all only supportive service any one who wishes to avail these services must have thorough knowledge about the ways and means of gathering these assistance. I sincerely say that the Entrepreneur are playing vital role in development of rural area. He is the key part in development not only for the rural area but also for the country's economy be an entrepreneur become a tool for our economy growth.

21

Entrepreneurship Management Concepts and Information Technology

Mrs. Chitra Jeya Murugan

Introduction

Information Technology is broad term covering all aspects of managing and processing information. Computer hardware, software and Internet are the key to these systems that are designed, developed, supported or managed by Information Technology professionals. The development of Information Technology is one of the most significant achievement of the twentieth century. The role of Information Technology as an instrument for progress and development has been acknowledged widely and is expected to bring in major social and economic benefits for the mankind and accelerate the process of development. Information Technology can make greater impact on electronic governance, modernization of the office environment, crime detection, telemedicine etc.

Besides, the computer hardware and software, the other major component of Information Technology is the computer communication network. The present age is dominated by technology in which Information Technology by virtue of Information Technology meta resource nature is very influential. No aspect of life or service has been left untouched by Information Technology. This powerful tool has been instrumented in improving the performance of every sector where it is used. The best approach to utilize information technology in everyday life is to identify the areas where Information Technology can be applied and then to evolve a strategy to achieve it.

Entrepreneurship Management

One of the major applications of Information Technology for better quality of service to the citizen is Entrepreneurship management. Entrepreneurship management means practices and policies not only within the enterprise, but also practices and polices outside, in the market place.

Successful Entrepreneurial Management requires the following:

1. Market Analysis
2. Financial Planning
3. Efficient Management
4. Entrepreneurs Ability

The Information Technology industry has also created a new set of entrepreneur and also it is used in management activity of the entrepreneurship.

Market Analysis

Unless a new venture is totally market focused it will succeed only in creating an opportunity for a competitor. A new product creates a market than an old product. A business is paid to satisfy customers and improve the market. A market analysis is essential for testing a new venture. Market is not a geographical meeting place but as getting together of buyers and sellers in person, by mail, telephone, telegraphy, or any other means of communication.

Marketing is a human activity directed at satisfying needs and wants through an exchange process. The modern marketing is consuming market, we are in a position to satisfy the consumer. In the traditional marketing to satisfy the consumer is difficult one. But now-a-days it is very easiest one because of Information Technology. Application of Information Technology in the entrepreneurship development in the market place is known as Electronic market place.

Electronic Market Place

Electronic markets ordinarily refer to online trading markets, online auction for computers and other goods. The electronic market place refers to the emerging market economy where producer intermediaries and consumers interact electronically or digitally in some way. The electronic market place is a virtual representative of physical markets. The economic activities undertaken by this electronic market place collectively represent the digital economy. E-commerce broadly defined, is concerned with the electronic market place.

E-commerce

In olden days people were used to exchange the commodities depending upon their requirements and to call it as the commerce. In today's economic scenario the market place is increasingly global and competition the growth of Internet and web based technologies. Therefore the business process requires efficient co-ordination of information between suppliers and customers with the help of e-commerce the business will be transacted very fast. Without e-commerce, the result is delayed response and higher cost, resulting decreased customer satisfaction. Internet provides a faster information highway to transact business.

E-commerce is very useful in Entrepreneurship management in the way of conducting, managing and executing business transaction and services through electronic media and networks.

The ultimate purpose of e-commerce is to ensure better customer satisfaction. People all around the world can sit in the houses and can accomplish what they desire through a few mouse clicks and tabs on the keyboard. They can select their commodities through the multicolor catalogs. So the customer need not to face the problems in his purchase as "no stocks", "closing time" and flying long distance. It is also termed as e-business, e-shop, e-market and e-everything.

The different kinds of site are available for conducting e-commerce in the market fields are:

1. Direct selling
2. Product demonstration, and
3. Promotional activities.

Direct Selling

The small seller get a chance to compete against much bigger player in almost every field, e-commerce provide an opportunity to the people to come-out in contract with superior goods or superior pattern of consumption with the new articles. Entrepreneurs are able to start business more easily with smaller upfront investment requirement. Business to customer concept of e-commerce the products are directly sell to the end customer. An Entrepreneurship management using this e-commerce an entrepreneur sell their goods directly to the end customer.

Product Demonstration

An entrepreneurship management, any entrepreneur wants to purchase the raw material or any other goods, first they refer the quotation of various company, then they select the company and also go to that market place and verify about the goods. For the above activities it consumes more time, to avoid such things simply they use the information technology and in the on-line they see the product demonstration and also they compare the quotation of various companies and select their choice.

So the information technology reduce the time, cost and energy of entrepreneur in the entrpereneurship management.

Promotional Activities

E-commerce provides very easy way to get in touch with the customer at global level. Information technology produce high global instant visibility of the product through web technology and hence better product promotion. At relatively lower cost than magazine advertising, companies can use web for interactive advertisement and reach an international audience.

In the entrepreneurial management concept an advertisement is essential to make the entrepreneurs goods and services. So the entrepreneur can use the Information Technology for advertising their product.

Financial Planning

The right financial policies are required for the success of a new venture. Lack of initiative to raise the capital needed for expenses may lead to the collapse of business. Sound cash management are essential i.e. to less expenses and correct payments leads to efficient cash management.

Information Technology also involved in the financial planning. Information Technology plays a vital role in the financial transaction by two concepts.

1. Electronic cash
2. Digital money

Electronic Cash

Information Technology refers to one of the many schemes that permit a person to pay for goods and services by transmitting a number from one computer to a other. The number is given by the bank. In this case payment is made by the buyer and seller immediately.

Digital Money

Information Technology refers to grabbag term for the many electronic cash and payment scheme on the Internet. By using this scheme the buyer and seller make the payments immediately.

So the delivery of goods are made only after the receipt of money due for it. Thus the chance of bad debts are removed. Funds are received promptly and quickly.

The flow of funds are smart. So the expenditure of distribution and receipt of cash is economized. So Financial planning is well done with the help of Information Technology in entrepreneurship management.

Efficient Management

The successful operation of new venture in an entrepreneurship management requires an efficient management team and a team cannot be developed overnight. To identify the suitable member for the team, the membership should be allotted on the basis of their abilities are aptitudes.

An entrepreneurship management requires efficient management. First we have identify the correct person for a team. Before identification we are giving adverisement, receive the application form from candidates, and scrutiny the application like this more work are made, but now we simply gave advertisement in the internet and the application is sent by the candidates in the e-mail. So we have quickly identify the member easily with low cost.

In olden days the hierarchical system of management is one to one system. But now-a-days it is all to all systems. It is denoted the information technology concept is Management Information System (MIS).

Entrepreneurs Ability

Entrepreneurship management a successful entrepreneurs must be a person with technical competence, initiative, good judgment, energy, attitude, creativeness, fairness, honesty tactfulness and emotional stability.

Along with above ability he should possess the creative thinking and knowledge about information technology.

A survey conducted in Mexico revealed that 2/3 of small scale entrepreneur were using computer, and 44% of the group have access to the internet.

Entrepreneurs in the developing countries like India can secure gain from information technology with little technical training.

In a remote village in Guyana women formed an organization called rupumuni weavers society to revive the ancient art of hand weaving large hammocks from locally grown cotton. Then they marketed hand woven hammocks over the Internet to people all over the world at a price of $1000 each: which is enormous comparer to local standards.

The best known of the Information Technology enabled business story is the case of grameen phones in Bangladesh. Grameen bank promotes micro enterprises among women through a wholly owned subsidiary called Grameen Telecom. It is enabled women to retail phone calls on their cellular phones. Village women can borrow enough money on loan from grameen bank to purchase a cell phone. Women who have been given cell phones can retain their cell phone. Services and they can pay back the loan with the revenues from the sale of phone calls.

Now-a-days most of the entrepreneurs are successful in their field, because of information technology. So the information technology plays vital role in the entrepreneurship management.

Conclusion

Information Technology plays vital role in the entrepreneurship management. First, marketing, they have used the e-commerce for purchasing, selling, promotional activity and payments. So in the marketing field Information Technology plays important role: then financial analysis electronic cash and digital money is applied to control the financial aspect: then management, in the management level selection, recruitment, placement, training and communication concepts involve Information Technology in the form of e-mail. Finally along with basic entrepreneurial ability a person must have possess knowledge about information technology. A single hand does not raise any sound. Similarly Information Technology alone cannot make wonders. Information Technology applied in the fields of commerce, economics, management chemistry, Biotechnology and entrepreneurship management can do magic in that respective fields.

22

Contact Management Solution and Entrepreneurship Management

Dr. R. Srinivasan

Background

During the decade of 1990s, an unprecedented growth has been experienced in some economies of the world. Many countries of the world joined the market economy. The world became more like a global village.

Information technology and knowledge based industries brought drastic changes in the system of transacting business. Foreign direct investment picked up and there was significant flow of funds from developed countries to lesser-developed and developing countries. The entire world was over-enthused about the role of information technology. The information technology bubble started bursting from the dawn of 21st century.

During the past one decade, many countries of the world have switched over from protected economic regime to market economy. Winds of liberalization, privatization and globalization are sweeping across the world as more and more nations are increasingly joining the bandwagon of free market economy

"Entrepreneurship skills are in high demand by competitive and profitable businesses striving to contend in today's dynamic global marketplace. Successful entrepreneurial ventures bring together a visionary leader, a committed team and a marketable idea."

Maintaining contact with people is a key success factor for entrepreneurs. This includes contact with prospects, customers, clients, vendors and suppliers. It is through these contacts that entrepreneur build the relationships that are so vital to their business. As a result, it is essential that entrepreneur make the most of these contacts. And the best way to do it is with effective contact management.

If entrepreneur work with only a few contacts, entrepreneur can probably manage the business relationships with a simple calendar and address book. If entrepreneur works with numerous contacts, however, entrepreneur need much more. Entrepreneur need an automated and efficient system to help entrepreneur manage contacts and related activities effectively so entrepreneur can maintain tight business relationships. Entrepreneur needs a contact management software solution.

Contact management solution is an *"indispensable tool"* for entrepreneurs. It is also an ideal solution for other business people are externally focused and working to build a business. Examples include small business owners, consultants, professional recruiters' etc.

What is Contact Management?

Contact management is the management of all the tasks and information related to developing and maintaining relationships with the people with whom entrepreneur does business. It involves a variety of activities, including:

- Identifying and contacting new prospects
- Following up with prospects and clients by telephone, fax, mail and e-mail

- Delivering product information, proposals, and quotes
- Scheduling appointments and meetings
- Creating correspondence to follow up and to generate new sales/Business.
- Managing customers' post sales requests for service and support
- Maintaining accurate records of all contact interactions
- Generating reports for reviewing activities and client/account status.

Difference between Contact Management Solution and other Interaction Solutions

A wide variety of products are available to help business people in dealing with others. Let's look at the difference between contact managers and two of the categories most closely related to contact managers: Personal information managers (PIMs) and Collaboration & Communication solutions, such as Microsoft Outlook.

Contact Managers

Contact managers are designed specifically for relationship driven professionals. Contact managers make these people more effective in managing relationships by helping them manage their interactions with people outside the organization. Interactions include contact with prospects, customers, clients, and business partners such as suppliers and distributors.

A comprehensive contact manager includes:

- Ready to use database with searching
- Notes and customizable fields
- A calendar that links to contacts

- Automatic History with notes
- Mail, fax and email merge
- Customized reporting
- Sales tools
- Links to the Internet
- Import/Export Utility

Built on the foundation of a contact-centric database, contact managers provide complete and comprehensive tracking of all the information related to contacts. For example, if a meeting is held with a particular contact, the contact manager tracks the meeting date and time, the subject, the attendees, all associated correspondence, and any meeting notes.

Contact managers add a user interface to the power of a database allowing fast and easy access to all information associated with a contact. When a client telephones, for example, a consultant can immediately display a complete contact history for that client, including proposals, schedules, contracts, meetings, and telephone calls. Contact managers also provide tools that automate routine communication and reporting activities.

Personal Information Managers (PIMs)

PIMs provide some of the capabilities of contact managers. However, there are important differences. A PIM is used primarily as an electronic record-keeping device that helps people move all their personal information onto their computers. It maintains information that has typically been scattered across a variety of paper devices such as index cards, Rolodexes, and calendars.

A PIM usually includes an address book, a calendar, and a to-do list, and typically mimics the paper-based versions of these tools. PIMs help business people organize their personal information such as schedules, tasks and addresses. Unlike contact managers, however, PIM contact tracking functionality is rudimentary. Another important difference is that there is little integration between the components of a PIM, that is, PIMs don't integrate contacts, calendars, tasks and correspondence generation. In addition, PIMs provide limited, if any, capability to attach free form notes to contact records.

In summary, although PIMs store some of the same information maintained by contact managers, the information is not linked to contacts. As a result, it is time-consuming to gather all the information related to a specific contact and therefore cumbersome to use a PIM for contact management.

Collaboration and Communication Solutions

Collaboration and communication solutions are designed primarily to help users organize information on the desktop and communicate and share this information among colleagues in a workgroup, department or team.

Collaboration and communications solutions typically include:

- Calendar
- Record keeping
- Email
- Task list
- Address book
- Document management

Communication solution is built on the integration of four components: email, a scheduling manager, an address book, and a document management capability. As a result, it is well suited for coordinating the activities of a work group or team in that it facilitates collaboration and communication within the group, and it provides document flow control.

In contrast, contact managers are usually built on a contact-centric database and are designed for day-to-day management of contact information in an individual or small group environment. A contact manager provides an excellent solution for people who work with outside contacts and need to keep track of all communications with each contact.

How Contact Management Solution Can Help Grow a Business

Whether entrepreneur the owner of a small business, a consultant or other externally focused professional, a Contact manager can help entrepreneur work more effectively in a variety of ways:

- It gives entrepreneur instant access to complete contact information—from addresses, phone numbers, and birthdays, to a comprehensive record of every interaction
- It helps entrepreneur manage his contacts more effectively
- It makes it easier to communicate with prospects and customers—whether entrepreneur want to contact them by telephone, mail, e-mail or fax
- It helps entrepreneur to analyze, understand and report the state of his business
- It brings the world of Internet technology to his customer database

With contact manager, he'll get more done everyday and he'll present a more organized and professional image to clients and prospects. The result is he'll build more, longer-lasting business relationships. And that 's the key to growing their business.

Conclusion

Contact managers were designed originally as powerful tools for entrepreneurs. However, as contact manages grew in capability, their value has become apparent to a much wider audience. That's because contact manager helps people manage their business relationships more effectively, whether they are entrepreneurs or other business professionals. And effective management of relationships is the key to growing a business.

"Build Contacts Create Visibilities"

23

Role of IT on Entrepreneurship Development

G. Vijay Jesuraj

Introduction

Indian Labour organization describes "Entrepreneurs are people who have the ability to see and evaluate business opportunities to gather the necessary resources to take advantage of them and to initiate appropriate action to ensure success."

Evolution of Entrepreneurship

The word entrepreneur first appeared in the French language and was applied to leaders of military expeditions in the beginning of 16th century. After 1700 it was applied to other types of adventures, mainly civil engineering like the construction of roads, bridges, harbours and buildings.

Richard Cantillon an Irish man living in France was the first person to use the term entrepreneur to refer to economic activities. According to him, entrepreneurs carry on production and exchange of goods at some risk facing the possibility of bankruptcy when the demand for their products is depressed.

Information Technology

Information Technology (IT) is the science of information handling, particularly by computers, used to support the communication of knowledge in social, economic and technical fields. It is the convergence of three strands of technology:

- Computing
- Microelectronics
- Telecommunications.

It is the combination of these three technologies, which promises so much for the future. The hardware aspects of IT would include devices such as computers, microprocessors, and communication lines. The Software aspects of IT would include operating systems, computer applications like spreadsheet and database management. It also includes robotics, computer integrated manufacturing, telecommunication, management information system and decision support system.

Importance of Information Technology

'Survival of the fittest' is the rule of our present competitive market economy and it is important that for a survival competitive edge over others are inevitable. Every piece of information gathered has its prominence and the more information a person acquires, greater is the competitive advantage. The only way suitable to gather it is the IT way.

Application of Information Technology

IT is redefining every facet of human life. The shape of things to come is increasingly being dictated by IT. The impact of IT can be seen in almost all walks of life. It is used extensively in the fields of research, business and industry, space technology, telecommunication, transportation. Public and business administration, health care, libraries and museums, defence and so on. It plays important role in recreation and entertainment and education and training. New branches of industry and training have emerged as IT industry and IT Education.

Components of Information Technology

Many organizations in our country have been using IT either for selected activities or for entire activities in their organisations. For managing any kind of business, primary requirement is information. No business can survive without internal and external information. IT facilitates to organize information for business process. It is a misconception to come to the conclusion that IT is melting, when it is not.

Information Technology and Entrepreneurship Development

In the late seventies and early eighties, when computers were introduced for data processing in organizations, it was feared that these computers would replace manpower in organizations. It was never thought that it would be useful for decision process in their business activities.

The systems model of management shows that each and every communication is needed for carrying out the managerial functions and for linking the entrepreneurship with its external environment. The management system has to be tailored to specific needs and may include routine information such as monthly reports, information points, exceptions, especially at critical points, and information necessary to predict the future.

Business is becoming highly competitive. Competition is arising not only from traditional markets, but also from entrants to specific industry or economic order. This has resulted in disintegration of barriers to previously insulated and protected markets. A new era has set in the business environment. Globalization, market useful for managing entrepreneurship. Entrepreneurs can use them for planning their business strategies, visualizing the possible scenario, analyzing the information with different alternatives and many more things for decision making and forming policies

1. ***Useful for Managing Enterpreneurship:*** Entrepreneurs can use them for planning their business strategies, visualizing the possible scenario, analyzing the information with different alternatives and many more things for decision making and forming policies that Data Mining is "a torturing of data base contents until they confess the secrets they hold". This is more useful for the entrepreneurs for analyzing and forecasting. This is also helps them in conducting research in any area in the business.

2. ***Simulation:*** It is a model which will respond to the information the user presents. It carries out calculations based on all the information it has. Results can be predicted for real life situations. It is the best concept that helps the management to test the ding enormous volumes of information in each and every fields of human knowledge. It is used by all category of peoples. Since it becomes the necessity of every human life, so also for the entrepreneurs also with the help of this the entrepreneurs can develop their business by giving their product details with the help of E-Commerce, which facilitates them of avoiding middlemen or brokers for their business. It also facilitates to exchange mail very fast with millions of people all over the world at very economical rates, much cheaper when compared to telephone.

The Entrepreneurs can also attract customers by giving advertisements through internet.

Conclusion

Control techniques and Information Technology are basically the same regardless of what is being controlled the basic control process involved in the Entrepreneurship development by way of establishing standards. Computers are now extensively used. Their impact on the development of Entrepreneurship differs. Information Technology provides many challenges. We should fortify our system by establishing links with foreign institutions of international excellence. Thus India should strive to develop and create the required human resources for IT and lead the IT Revolution and exploit fully the opportunities provided especially by the globalisation.

establishing links with foreign institutions of international excellence. Thus India should strive to develop and create the required human resources for IT and lead the IT revolution and exploit fully the opportunities provided especially by the globalisation.